Windrows

Harvesting the Lessons of Life

DENNIS L. VAN HAITSMA, PHD

Graphics/Art by Julie Sweers

ISBN: 978-1-4834-3903-7 (sc)
ISBN: 978-1-4834-3902-0 (e)

Lulu Publishing Services rev. date: 2/24/2016

Contents

Foreword

WHILE I CHOSE NOT TO be a farmer by profession, I was raised as one, by two who were. And although I think I have long ago given up many of my childhood as well as my "farmer-ish" ways, I am often reminded how much I have been and continue to be influenced having lived my earlier days on a farm. We are who we were, and we will be who we are; past meets present, present meets future. No doubt, my friends would probably enter me as "Exhibit A" when it comes to proving that there is more than a kernel of truth in the saying, "You can take the boy out of the farm, but you can't take the farm out of the boy." So it only makes sense that the things I experienced in my life on the farm would not only serve as the springboard for so many of my memories, but those same experiences would continue to influence my life now and into my future. In honor of my past and in recognition of its impact on my present, I have titled my memoirs *Windrows*. Since I realize this title might resonate more with those who understand farming than those who do not, allow me to explain the reason why I selected this title, and why I think it both honors my past and recognizes how my past has and continues to influence my present.

My siblings and I grew up with the "Waste not, want not!" adage ringing in our ears, a mentality my parents seemed to have shared "in spades" with many of their post-Depression peers. It was because of the Depression that we not only did a lot of things on our farm according to the practices of those days, but we often seemed to go above and beyond in our attempts to be downright penny-pinching frugal. Take haying, for example. It was the practice back then to mow a field and let the cuttings lie for a day or two after which we would use a piece of equipment called a side-delivery rake, its constructed function being such that when pulled by a tractor over the initial cutting, it would rake and roll the swaths of mowed hay into rows commonly known as "windrows." In this spiraled configuration, the hay would not only dry more quickly in the sun and breezes, it could also be harvested more quickly and efficiently. When it would finally be determined, by those more adept at making such determinations, that the hay was dry enough to be gathered and stored in the barn as food or bedding for the cattle, the "haying" would begin. Failure to allow the hay to dry sufficiently would often result in its molding at best or sparking spontaneous combustion at worst. Every once in awhile, our local newspaper would carry a "reminder" story of a barn burned to the ground due to overly anxious harvesters; while every farmer in the area knew the details surrounding such fires often before the newspaper would report them, it was always something every farmer dreaded might happen to their own barn if they were not vigilant.

At such time as the hay would finally be declared dry enough to be harvested, a convoy led by a tractor pulling a wagon dragging a hay-loader behind it could be seen heading for the field. With the tractor following the windrow, the hay-loader would auger the wind-rowed hay up and unto the wagon where the hay would be loaded and eventually brought to the barn and stored for use as needed. In the truest sense of the "waste not, want not" adage, my dad would go one step further. To ensure that every possible blade of hay was harvested, after the initial removal of windrows was accomplished, Dad would then employ the use of a piece of equipment known as a dump-rake. Attached to the tractor, this piece of equipment would then be pulled back and forth against the grain of the initial windrow. Combing the field in this fashion into makeshift windrows would pretty much ensure the collection of any errant blades of grass that might have escaped the side delivery rake. Once the dump-raking was accomplished, the convoy of tractor and hay-loader would return to the field for one last round of harvesting. This typically resulted in our fields being swept as clean as a church in preparation for its Sunday morning service. While I can assure you that it was never my intent to bore anyone with a clean sweep of my past, fearing that such a complete airing would merely result in dry prose, I did attempt to gather up stories from my past that were significant to me, if for no other reason than I remember them. My hope is that not only will these stories prove interesting for anyone who might decide to read them, but that they will also help those who knew me to know me better.

I admit that up until just recently these musings were just that—musings: stories, orally told, intended to entertain family and friends on those occasions when their telling appropriately fit into the gist of the conversation. But my more recent desire to revisit my past intentionally took root on the day I happened to witness the disappointment of my daughter. She had asked her grandmother (my mother) if she would be willing to write about some of her memories so that my daughter's own children might come to know and better understand something about their great-grandmother and about life in her time, but as it was, my daughter's request fell on deaf ears. Perhaps it was my mom's typical humility and/or her perceived complexity of the undertaking that prompted her to reply, "Oh, there's really nothing to tell."

Right then and there, I vowed to myself that my own grandchildren and those who will follow after them would have an opportunity to know about me if and whenever they might be curious or interested enough to want to know. It was only as I began culling the past for the things that might be of interest to them, that I have come to realize my efforts were more than merely a nostalgic glance back over my shoulder, more than merely an attempt to "rake" and align as many pieces of my memory as possible into some sort of meaningful whole. As things continued to progress, it became apparent to me that actually I was rediscovering myself. By pausing to look back, I am seeing how my past is so much my present.

Given that, let us start up the tractor, hitch up the rake, and head across the fields to gather up some remembrances and expose them to the light of day, with the idea in mind that by doing so, someone might reap some benefit in this undertaking.

Acknowledgements

I T IS WITH HEARTFELT APPRECIATION that I tip my hat to those who helped make these stories possible. Thanks goes out to my parents who did the very best they could to help make my life better than their own. It goes without saying that I should also acknowledge my two brothers who each in their own way helped to shape me and in some instances to "shape me up." And as I look back, there is very little doubt in my mind that my third brother, who died before I was born, in some ways influenced my life as well.

A mitt-full of thanks also goes out to my own family and especially my two children—Kimberly and Brad—as well as all the teachers and pastors from my past who influenced me in numerous ways even though their exact contributions to my development are not always clear. I also owe a debt of gratitude to my life-long mentor and friend Ron VanderSchaaf, who always encouraged me to continue my writing and to my very dear friend Julie Sweers, who not only cheered me on, edited my drafts, and proofread the final text, but also provided the illustrations found in this book.

And finally, thanks goes out to my Holland, Michigan south-side *McDonald* friends who tolerated my occupying a booth for hours on end while downing more coffee than any patron deserved to be served in one sitting even though I kept assuring them that when the book was finished they would receive a copy. Well gang, the book is finally finished; fortunately, my life continues.

Disclaimer

WHILE IT IS NOT ALWAYS in one's best interest to apologize up front, allow me to risk making two confessions. First, even though I had intended in placing these memoirs in some sort of chronological order, you will soon discover that I have not done a very good job of that. My hope is that each chapter will be able to stand on its own.

Second, very little is written today that does not include some fine print at the bottom of the page. Wanting to be up front with you as well as personal, I feel it is important to remind you that what you are about to read are *my* memoirs, written as they are from *my* memory. Quite likely those who claim to already know a lot about me will read these memoirs and perhaps find something to decry as being inaccurate according to their memories. To those who might find themselves in this camp, I would urge you to write *your* own memoirs.

THE EARLY YEARS

ONE

School Days

The difference between school and life? In school you're taught a lesson and then given a test. In life, you're given a test that teaches you a lesson.

-Tom Bodett

MY FORMAL SCHOOLING BEGAN IN 1950 housed in a two room building designed for that purpose and located at the opposite end of our mile. I recall that its classrooms always smelled of a musty ancientness that seemingly hung in the air suspended somewhere between the high ceilings and the well worn plank floors. These floors supported rows of small sledded desks, each scared by years of bored carvings, innocent first loves, and unattended stains. Adding to the aura were chalk dusted, slate blackboards that clung relentlessly to poorly patched and repainted plaster walls bearing pictures of Dwight D. Eisenhower and all of the past presidents along with perfectly scripted letters of the entire alphabet. Periodically, as strange as it might seem to those not inclined to spend a lot of time thinking on such things, these smells and a plethora of others still activate my recollections of those earlier days. I am not exactly sure how I got to be wired this way, leaving me to wonder if this acute hyperosmia is just a part of my divine design or if it is just something I acquired as a result of my being nurtured on a farm. Pinpointing its exact origin and onset would certainly take a lot more thought and time than I am willing to give to it; besides, I am pretty sure that such an exact determination would be of little value anyway. Long ago, I resigned myself to just accept and appreciate this ability.

Many of my favorite recollections of early schooling revolved around those rare occasions when we would be the recipients of a brand new text or workbook. Whenever such was the case, two events would occur in sequence as surely as "B" follows "A." First, as a class, we would be required to properly break-in our new book by subjecting it to a series of bends and folds as prescribed by the manufacturer and strategically orchestrated by our teacher; and second, perhaps because growing up in a family more inclined toward second-hand and hand-me-downs, something almost instinctively would drive me to bury my nose into its spine and there inhale deeply of its newness. I would remain in this posture until, growing too uncomfortable with the looks emanating from my fellow classmates, I would lift my head pretending to be oblivious to their perplexed stares. Even now, much less concerned with what others might think, I take literally the figurative notion of "burying one's nose in a book." While many years later someone stumbled onto the fact that the glue used to hold books together could, in fact, serve multiple purposes, I can assure you that my intentions then, as well as now, were purely innocent albeit sensual.

A new box of crayons runs a close second in setting off incidents of recall. And even though I seldom possessed such a luxury of my own, I was always less than shy when it came to asking my more affluent classmates if I could borrow theirs, not for their rainbow of options, mind you, nor for the precision they could lend my efforts to color inside the lines made all the easier by their unworn tips, but rather for the occasion to breathe in the scent they afforded. Freshly sharpened pencils, paste, industrial strength floor and furniture polish, as well the contents of our ink wells, all can be found among the smorgasbord of smells that can transport me back to those earlier days, leaving me to deduce that perhaps my elementary schooling is where this propensity for the odiferous all began.

Miss Thompson, who taught grades kindergarten through second grade, was my introduction to formal schooling. She was considered, by those who felt it necessary to voice their opinion on such matters, "a plain Jane." I do not recall that she emitted any really memorable smells; in fact, she seemed to blend in quite well with the rest of us kids except on those very warm days when her excessive poundage would combine with the heat to produce smells familiar to those of us more accustomed to working in the fields on those sweltering dog-days of summer. However, I do recall one feature about her that was quite memorable. Even at my young age, I could not help but notice that she displayed rather large bosoms, the cleavage of which she was never modest or kempt enough to consider covering in the presence of such impressible pre-pubescents. Consequently, when she would hug you, which she often did, especially when you had performed well or needed some consoling to ease a hurt, all the lights would go out, and darkness would prevail until such time as she saw fit to release you.

Mrs. Hunter, who taught grades three through five, on the other hand, stood out in stark contrast. Considered a fastidious dresser topped off with perfectly coiffed blue gray hair and large earrings, she would more typically shower you with deserved praise while keeping her distance. Even though "neat as a pin" and "dressed to the nines" aptly described her, her painted face and fingernails made her suspect in our conservative community. Fortunately, as children, we were shielded from such grist for the gossip-mill, but I am absolutely certain that had I somehow become privy to her alleged dark side, it would have made no difference to me because she always smelled so good. Despite our never being able to gain close proximity to her, I still detected that every part of her tended to radiate aromas blending *Lilies of the Valley* and *Evening in Paris* perfumes with an underbody of *Dial* soap. I can only imagine, from my present perspective, how difficult it must have been for her to be stuck in a rural school far away from those of her kind; and I chuckle at the irony that most of the kids she taught came directly to school from the barn where *Lava* soap, showers, or baths were things typically relegated to Saturday nights, whether they were needed or not, so one could be ready and in good form for Sunday. (No doubt this gave the local pastors a false sense of their young parishioners more typical hygienic practices.) I am convinced our lack of cleanliness is what eventually prompted Mrs. Hunter to add a health class to our school's curriculum.

As for Miss Thompson, perhaps it had something to do with her size that no one thought to question or bothered to question why she was single, but there was always a cloud swirling around Mrs. Hunter and how she had allegedly lost her husband in the war. Years later I discovered that such an explanation was often used in an effort to lessen the stigma of a married woman, now single, who might actually have lost her husband to alcoholism, divorce, or insanity. To my knowledge, a final verdict was never reached in the case of Mrs. Hunter's widowhood.

I do not recall that the daily mile walk to and from school to bask in these interesting smells was uphill both ways, but I do remember walking to school on many a blustery winter day and sinking well over my knees in snow banks, structures amplified by the fact that the road was vulnerable to drifting due to the open fields that bordered it on both sides. To make matters even more interesting, our road was typically among the last to be plowed, which greatly restricted vehicular transportation until well into the late afternoon. Like pioneers, we were usually the first to leave tracks in the newly fallen snow. Admittedly, my knees were a bit closer to the ground back then, but that fact does not detract from the depth of snow we trudged through in order to receive our education. Such trekking to and from school would result not only in my experiencing the discernible smells of icy cold air served up against the backdrop of azure skies brush-stroked by white wisps of smoke emitting from the chimneys of houses with coal and wood-burning furnaces, but also the smells unique to wet denim. Despite my bibbed overalls having had numerous previous encounters with Mom's homemade lye and lard soap, they always seemed mysteriously capable of producing blue legs, which served to further witness my encounter with the elements.

Because school cancellations were not yet a luxury of broadcasts, and party-lines not yet a staple in our neighborhood, unless Mom deemed the weather to be too treacherous and declared it "not fit for man nor beast," we would bundle up and traverse the tundra that spread out between our home and the school.

On more than one occasion, we would arrive only to find a note tacked to the entrance door of our school that read, "Due to the inclement weather, school is cancelled for today." While no one of our age group knew what the word "inclement" meant, we all understood the meaning of "school is cancelled for today," so we would turn around and trudge back home, all the while planning the many ways we would take advantage of our unexpected parole.

I recall one particular day when "Punkie," my nearest neighbor friend and often fellow traveler to and from school, got into trouble. Having arrived at school earlier than most that day, he tacked just such a cancellation notice to the front door. Those kids who could read only read the part about school being cancelled for the day and half of them had already left for home before two very upset teachers discovered the devious act. It was Punkie's discernible handwriting, as well as his misspelling of the word "inclement," that indicted him. Rumor had it that this little indiscretion resulted in his being relegated to "solitary confinement" in the coal bin located in the school's creepy basement where, for an undetermined period of time, he was to make his atonement. Only later did it surface that he had actually undergone a tonsillectomy that kept him out of school for two weeks, where upon his return, Miss Thompson must have felt sorry for him because he emerged from her consoling darkness free of any required explanation or penance.

Even the scent of a struck match will spark a memory of my early school days. I recall the day I had strategically launched a rubber-banded paper wad, smack dab into the ear of a freckled-faced redhead named Molly. I admit it was a childish thing to do, but how else does one tell a girl that you sort of like her when you are only ten years old? Not only did Molly decline my overture of affection, she also "told on me," which led to a swift conviction – a sentence that required me to serve three in-door recesses as well as lose my after-school trash and paper burning privileges for a month. This was a coveted chore among my peers in that it legitimized playing with fire, a definite no-no under every other circumstance. While I was so hoping that my innocent inappropriateness would, in fact, convey to Molly that I wanted her to be my girl, it all backfired on me. Having her finger me as the culprit was not nearly as painful as her adding insult to what I already considered to be an injury of unrequited love by continuing to reign down scornful looks in my direction for many months thereafter, leaving me to conclude that not only were my feelings for her unreciprocated, perhaps this boy-girl stuff had more to do with smoke than fire.

The odor of a musty refrigerator still stimulates a recollection of yet another school chore. This chore involved the noon retrieval of milk cartons from the cooler located in the school's basement, a job Mrs. Hunter saw fit to assign only to the older boys and then only those whom she judged capable of handling the heavy plastic crate used to transport the pint-sized cardboard capped glass milk bottles of Vitamin D to the first floor. This was another of those coveted assignments we considered ourselves fortunate to be assigned to and unfortunate when our turn came to an end. I am not sure Mrs. Hunter fully realized that by assigning us to this task she was also bestowing on us the title of "he-man." Being someone capable of wheeling such a heavy transport, we felt would surely place us in good stead with the girls. But there was another reason for our coveting this particular assignment. It was known only to the boys who actually had been assigned to the task and shared with a few select others who we felt were capable of adhering to the code of life-long secrecy.

During the summer months prior to the start of my fifth grade experience, our school had undergone a modernization which saw a portion of the coal bin converted into an indoor restroom for the girls, thanks, in part, to the generosity of some local bigwig donating a used boiler from his business which made the coal bin obsolete. The boys, meanwhile, were still required to use the outhouse, or with trusted look-outs manning their posts, any other discreet outdoor structure or foliage. To the relief of those more inclined toward misbehavior, the remodeling of the coal bin confirmed the fact that it could no longer be used as a maximum security facility, for it was rumored (ever since Punkie's mysterious disappearance) that it would be reserved for those who might transgress beyond a teacher's patience.

The plywood wall construction now separating the relocated milk cooler from the girls' newly installed restroom just happened to feature a knothole that nature had seen fit to make more a hole than a knot, seemingly affording anyone who would peer through it a glimpse of whoever might be using the facility on the other side. I recall my disappointment in being able to only see the stall's ceiling owing to the fact that the hole was located in such a position that one would have to be well over six feet tall in order to take any sort of advantage of its potential. But that fact did little to restrict the flow of stories we boys would conjure up in vain attempts to one-up the more recent and decadent ones being told.

The smell of disinfectant conjures up memories of the day that, while horsing around at recess time, I "kneed" a fellow classmate. To successfully complete a kneeing, one is required to sneak up on an unsuspecting victim (never a female) from behind, and while grabbing their shoulders, bring one's knee up to make a convincing contact with that person's buttock. Although I now realize such activity had absolutely no redeeming qualities short of passing the time, it was just one of the things we did back then to entertain ourselves during free time; after all, it was well before the advent of ipods, cell phones, and video games. On this particular occasion, my victim let out a blood curdling scream, and as he fled in the direction of the school entrance, I could not help but notice the seat of his slacks quickly turning a bright red. Stunned and unable to understand what had just happened, I felt the weight of my classmates' stares as if they had already convicted and sentenced me for what I had in my head already considered to be a grave crime, perhaps one bordering on premeditated murder.

I recall when the bell rang signaling the end of the recess period, instead of heading into school with the rest of my classmates, I headed for the field that bordered our playground, seeking to make contact with God, intending to barter with Him in such a way that if He would let my classmate live, I would right all the wrongs I had ever committed and avoid all those I had not yet had occasion to even consider committing. Sitting there in that field camouflaged like a wood duck in tall grass and wanting so much to be taken up, I heard Mrs. Hunter call my name. She urged me to show myself, all the while assuring me that my errant behavior would not be life-threatening. I later learned that my victim suffered from a boil on his backside, and the pressure that was brought to bear on it from my kneeing, had caused it to burst open. While it was not a pleasant experience for either of us, a disinfectant laden bandage placed him on the road to healing. I, on the other hand, was a long time on the road to recovery. Even to this day, I feel an occasional tinge of guilt each time I find myself unsuccessful in upholding my end of the bargain I had made there among the weeds and wild flowers so many years ago.

Somewhere I read that not only does smell serve to stimulate recall, it is actually the last sense to leave us as we age. And as if that were not enough to convince us of its importance, somehow scientists have been able to determine that we actually choose our mates based on smell. Maybe there are some lucky ones who already know how to utilize this strategy, but as for the rest, given its elevated importance, it would certainly seem appropriate to offer a premarital course as a part of the high school curricula nurturing such an ability as opposed to just leaving everything to chance. While ignoring the facts does not change them, I doubt seriously such an intentional offering will ever be the case anytime soon. Meanwhile, perhaps the best we can hope for is a long life filled with good memories and a spouse who always smells good to us.

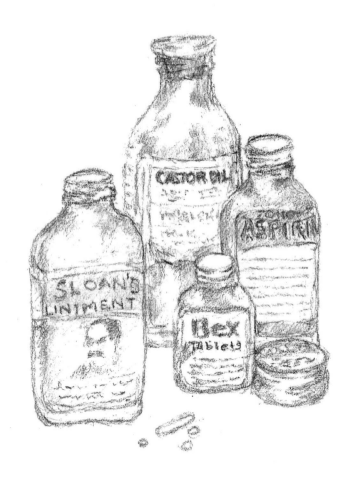

TWO

Home Remedies

Desperate maladies require desperate remedies.
-French Proverb

THERE IS A LOT ABOUT my recall of earlier events, especially those that occurred between the ages of birth to five years of age, that I confess might border on guessing or hearsay at best, but I am pretty confident I am not unique in my inability to conjure up some clear and flawless remembrances from those times. And as for those who claim they possess perfect recall, I am more than a bit suspicious as to whether they truly know of what they speak or if they have become convinced of it by the mere repetition of their own stories. Suffice it to say, I tend to liken those who claim such powers to Mark Twain's view on the matter. He once boasted his memory was so good he could recall things that did not even happen.

Yet every once in a while, I will have a vivid flashback prompted by a mindless TV show, an informal reading, or a casual encounter or conversation. The latter was the case most recently. It came on the heels of a visit I made to an elderly woman in the condo complex in which I live. Married for the first time at age fifty-eight to a sixty-five year old gentleman recently widowed, she and her husband had lived happily together for twenty-three years. His recent passing had lingered on the heels of his long and arduous struggle with major health issues during which time she was his constant caregiver and bedside companion. This particular conversation eventually lapsed into our talking about old fashioned remedies and how they more often than not would do the trick despite their unorthodoxy... and I was taken back to a time when, as a young child, my parents faithfully adhered to and practiced some pretty "unconventional" remedies of their own.

My mom would tell me how, when I was very young, I would often become quite sickly, especially during some of those Michigan winters. Rheumatic fever was a term bantered about in reference to my condition, and although I do not think I ever really contracted it, I often made my acquaintance with some of its very close relatives. Cough and croup seemed to always teeter on pneumonia—another medical diagnosis I recall hearing at a very young age—and while I associated it with something bad, it was not until some years later that I came to fully understand the gravity of its potential.

During those times when one of these maladies would hold me firmly in its grip, one of my parents' favored responses would be to generously rub *Vicks Vapor Rub* on my neck and chest as I was preparing for bed. They would then wrap a very hot cloth followed by a dry one around my neck which would then be safety-pinned ever so tightly to secure both in place for the night. This neck brace-like contraption they referred to as a "wet sock." If the situation proved to be even more critical, my parents would drape a bed sheet or blanket over my bed so as to form a tent-like canopy, its purpose being to help capture the steam from a vaporizer they used in order to ease my breathing through swollen tonsils and stuffed-up nostrils. Mom has often reminded me how the wallpaper would become so moist that it would loosen and curl. In fact, on more than one occasion, entire strips of wallpaper would find their way to the floor during the night, requiring some strategic re-pasting and replacing in the morning. After

I had grown much too old to feel threatened by this information, Mom confessed that on more than a few of those nights, there were serious doubts that I would survive to see the light of a new day.

To add insult to injury, illnesses of these sorts typically resulted in my parents coercing me to endure one or more of their diabolical remedies for such things. For sore throats, Mom would select a feather from the chicken coup, which she would clean and then dip into kerosene. While Dad would hold me down and pry open my mouth, Mom would "paint" my tonsils with the tip of the kerosene-soaked feather. I recall gagging and struggling like mad, so I assumed it was not any fun for my parents either, but they remained religiously convicted that this was for my own good. I was never clear as to how they came to know this information since at that time Mom had little time to read anything other than the Bible and the *Prairie Farmer*, and Dad read even less.

I later learned that the person my parents referred to as "our doctor" had assured them that this was the cheapest and best over-the-counter sore throat remedy on the market. While we seldom actually visited this doctor, I remember hearing my parents discuss the fact that they went to him because his fees were the most reasonable and his remedies made sense. I recall that the doctor's "office" where he met his patients consisted of one-room sparsely furnished and devoid of a receptionist or nurse. The office walls bore the names and telephone numbers of his patients along with the dates of their most recent visits and coded diagnoses. I recall looking at those walls and thinking of all those poor souls who were having their throats painted with kerosene because he would recommend it as the most economical and efficient way to address sore throats.

My parents' medical practice was not all about treating the symptoms. They were also firm believers in prevention as well, and to that end they became convinced of the preventive attributes of raw cod liver oil. Whether we kids needed it or not, their resolve was a spoonful a day of the "straight stuff." Some years later a flavored variety made its debut, which though that made swallowing it a bit easier, it only slightly reduced the embarrassing reminders that you had downed a spoonful of it earlier in the day. Even now, as much as I love to fish and eat what I catch, there cannot even be the slightest hint of a cod liver oil taste in the fish that I prepare. For this reason, I have come up with my own secret recipe that makes fish taste more like chicken (despite my aversion to feathers) which has also enamored me to the likes of bluegill or perch over salmon or steelhead any day of the week or year!

The sunlamp was also a mainstay preventive home remedy. A half-hour of absorbing its rays and warmth was a routine event especially during those cold winter months. I recall overhearing that it had something to do with the prevention of rickets or polio, but such a regime along with my dark hair often caused some confusion about my heritage. And while I grew to appreciate the added benefit of a nice bronze aura, I would lie there reluctantly because as an active young boy, giving up a half-hour of play time to stare with eyes closed up at a light seemed to be a senseless exchange for good health and an equally senseless waste of good play time.

And then there was *Nutra-Lite;* it, too, was considered a preventive measure. One of my uncles sold the product and expended little energy in convincing my parents of its value in warding off those sicknesses that seemed to be intent on pursuing little children and especially me. It required my downing a daily dosage of three "horse" pills. I recall watching my uncle's sales presentation which, while convincing my parents, only served to confuse me. Because of all the grain and alfalfa used in its composition, it seemed his sales pitch would be more appropriate as a commercial for farm feed. Somehow, I survived these pills and a whole host of other humongous capsules, whose origins and purposes I never did fully comprehend, combined with a variety of seltzers and teas equally mysterious, as well as an assortment of *Bag Balm, Camphor Oil, Iodine, Corn Huskers Lotion, Mother Gray Powder,* sweet oils, salt water, poultices, carbonated water, ad nauseam. Looking back, I had to admit that all these things combined must have done the trick because my attendance record, from the sixth grade through four years of college, was perfect! I did not miss a single day for physical health reasons or cut a single class for mental health reasons! Some might think that is because I did not have anything better to do, and they may have been right. But I must confess that the first year of my teaching career (sixth grade at Longfellow Elementary School in Holland, MI in 1968-69), I was sick and out of school all fifteen days allotted new teachers for such. I finished strong, though, claiming no sick days for the final twenty-two years of my career which allowed me to accumulate the maximum number of sick days allowed by contract, days that not only went unused and unremunerated, but also unrecognized! Oh well....

While it is true no one lives forever, the next best thing would seem to be to live more days healthy than not. To that end, I continue watching my diet and exercising, taking a regime of vitamins and minerals, daily eating multiple servings of fruits and vegetables and drinking sufficient quantities of water (mostly in the form of coffee); subconsciously, perhaps, I do all this in an effort to stay as far away from those kerosene soaked feathers as possible.

THREE

Play

It doesn't matter how old you are...if a little kid shoots you with a toy gun, you die on the spot.

-Unknown

GROWING UP ON OUR EIGHTY-ACRE farm, intended to sustain a family of five, kept us three young boys on a pretty tight work schedule, and yet my younger brother (two-and-a-half years my junior) and I always managed to eke out some time to satisfy most of our playful boyhood fantasies. As long as I can remember, my older brother (five years my senior) seldom involved himself in our play. Though the verdict as to why this might have been the case remains on the family docket, it seemed that if it were not about winning or making extra cash, it was merely a frivolous endeavor to him – a majoring in the minors– certainly not something worth his time or effort. Like the turtles my younger brother and I would rescue from the creek, our older brother appeared to be content living within the protective shell of these self-imposed intentions. Beleaguered by such adult-like cravings and burdened with the insatiable demands of first-born responsibilities, it was said that even before his face appeared to require a razor, his thinking and actions rivaled that of someone well beyond his years. My younger brother and I, on the other hand, whenever the lulls would allow, could be found immersed in frivolous play.

On any given day, the two of us could be seen utterly engrossed in building elaborate virtual multi-acred farms in our sandbox. Fortunately, the sandbox was shaded by a huge black walnut tree, which unfortunately also made playing there a bit precarious, especially in the fall, when its fruit would hail down on us unannounced, some dropping by nature, others by forging squirrels, who in their haste would occasionally mishandle their winter supply. Our sandbox farm, tractors, and select machinery were scaled-down life-like gifts from Christmases past. Our barns, animals, and fences were also usually store-bought or scrounged from someone else's discards. When all else failed, we would try our hand at construction, and if we lacked the skill or necessary materials for that, we would just fill in the gaps using our imagination.

Our harvested hay, for instance, would be grass extracted from our yard which always provided us with an endless supply. Once a week my younger brother and I would struggle with the old steel-wheeled reel mower, one pushing and mushing while the other, harnessed in a clothesline rope, did the pulling. Occasionally, the pushing would outdo the pulling, resulting in the mower riding up on the heels of the one out front. Whenever that would happen, our progress would inevitably be slowed a great deal and our time for play shortened, both byproducts of the boardroom-like negotiating and "hands on the Bible-like" promises which were required to ensure a non-reoccurrence of such painful experiences. Needless to say, it took awhile before we both felt comfortable enough to resume or reverse our roles.

Our harvested oats and wheat were also products of the lawn. To differentiate them from the hay, we would meticulously tie wads of grass into tiny bundles to resemble the harvesting mode of the day using thread taken from Mom's bounteous supply of spools neatly skewered in the thread box near her pedal sewing machine, which long ago had taken up permanent residence in the corner of our already too crowded dining room. Because the constructions of scaled down life-like binders and thrashing machines were not yet a reality, nor would they ever be the inventions of toy companies, we pretended that these bundles were being produced by imaginary machines. When these "bundles" would eventually be taken apart and "thrashed" by an equally imaginary thrashing machine, we would pitch the "straw" into the loft of our barn while with handfuls of actual wheat and oats, pilfered from Dad's granary, we would fill our small soup-can storage bins. To keep our "corn" from looking too much like our hay and straw, we would meticulously "chop" our "corn" into smaller bits and pieces using a pair of Mom's scissors. We would then store these cuttings as "silage" in our "silos" which conveniently were the construct of discarded cans of pork-and-beans.

When all the crops were finally harvested, we would commence plowing our fields and disking them into elaborate geometric designs that would have been the envy of any artistic farmer or mystic. When it would rain or our harvestings would begin to give off the tell-tale odors of mold and mildew, we would start all over again with even grander visions of farms and fields, undauntedly optimistic that the next planting and harvesting would be the best ever. I can only imagine how our parents must have felt as they sat around the kitchen table sipping their afternoon coffee and watching us through the window as our play validated their chosen occupation.

Sometimes when we would get bored with farming or come to a good stopping place, we could quickly transform our sandbox into an elaborate battlefield lined with strategically placed and partially hidden cowboys and Indians, figurines extracted from our *Fort Apache* set. Because we were not fussy, if neighborhood kids wanted to enlist their own figurines in the skirmish, it would not be uncommon to have coon-capped pioneers with their musket guns fighting alongside lance bearing knights, or helmeted soldiers wielding semi-automatic rifles and bazookas facing off against the always outnumbered Indians.

Tossing small stones and adding appropriate sound effects to replicate whizzing bullets and knifing arrows, we would commence our battles. When struck by one of these missiles, the figurine would topple over, actualizing its untimely demise. Occasionally, when the strafing failed to favor the side we wanted to win, when the battle needed to be cut short for dinner, or when we needed to promptly respond to "back-to-work" orders, we would drop "bombs" to speed things up. So it was that whenever we would eventually leave the "battlefield," we left it laden with carcasses in various stages of rigor mortis all semi-buried in moon-like craters beneath large stones.

Such warfare would often evolve into more life-sized adventures. In these roles, we could be seen "galloping" along the cow-worn pasture trails on stately steeds elaborately named, or we might be seen slinking behind the out buildings or underbrush, positioning ourselves to ambush the Indians or bad guys we imagined imposing grave threats to our livelihood. Our hardware often was a gun and holster set bearing the name of *Roy Rogers* or *The Lone Ranger*, the booty of fulfilled special-day wishes. But just as easily our hardware could be a no-longer-functioning squirt gun, a handle-less BB-gun, an abandoned or confiscated broom, a whittled stick, or anything else that did not require too much imagination for it to become something other than its original intent. Often these objects we would find while rummaging through the city dump which for us boys was a virtual toy store.

Whenever my folks visited our friends' parents, whose home happened to be strategically located near the dump's entrance, we kids, ignoring parental precautions concerning the rats and hidden diseases lurking there, would sneak into the dump. If we were successful in by-passing Mr. Yost, the dump's custodian who always managed to look right at home amidst the rubble, our visits never failed to spark fantasies the grandeur of which would be the envy of any mad scientist or Hollywood movie producer.

We considered ourselves fortunate and envied by all the neighborhood kids because our homestead featured a couple of outbuildings that had fallen into disuse. Our favorite "hang-out" was a brooding coup located in our orchard, the trees of which, because they were victimized by the lack of attentive pruning, spraying, and fertilizing, only produced multiple miniature bug-infested apples. In this abandoned coop, we would construct saloon-like conditions as seen on TV Westerns. As it was, since no one in our immediate family indulged in the spirits, the bottles and cans displayed on the shelves of our "saloon" were the products of whatever could be found that somewhat resembled the real thing. Occasionally, we would be fortunate enough to come across some actual discarded beverage containers along the road that passed by our house, but if we decided to add them to the wares of our establishment, we knew that we would have to keep them well hidden from our parents' view if we wanted to avoid yet another lecture on the evils of the "Devil's brew." As it was, because of Mom's particular aversion to anything that smacked of alcohol, it was a lot less stressful for us to use such things as discarded bottles of vanilla, molasses, medicine, syrup, or anything else that might transmit a sense of realism.

Our saloon was the scene of many imaginary brawls and the witness of numerous "show downs" featuring gun slingers intent on proving their skills and taking over our town. Fortunately, the good guys always managed to outdraw even the fastest outlaws in the West... or the East for that matter. While we could seldom convince anyone to actually play the roles of the bad guys, they were real to us, nonetheless. Occasionally, however, my younger brother would relent and take a bullet for the sake of realism because we both determined that his final gaspings were every bit as real as those emanating from someone unfortunate enough to have fallen at the hands of one of our heroes. When the dust finally settled and the episode concluded, we could be seen galloping off into the sunset on our imaginary steeds, confident that our town was safe and secure for yet another day, but equally convinced that our next adventure would be even more dangerously important than the one just completed.

Whenever we were not involved in actual or sandbox farming or playing cowboys and Indians, baseball held a particular fascination for us, perhaps because Dad was so into his *Cubs* and *White Sox*. Whenever the Christmas catalogs arrived and my brother and I would begin circling our desires, usually there was at least one baseball game targeted. Whether it was a pinball-like replica or a board game, none rivaled the make-believe elaborate baseball stadiums we would construct with large cardboard boxes, glue, paints and advertisements clipped from magazines destined to adorn our popsicle-stick outfield fences. Once erected, following a shortened version of the National Anthem, we would position the baseball cards of our favorite players on the field, and the game would commence using spit-laden cotton "baseballs" and sticks carved to replicate bats. By pre-determined design, but never acknowledged as an actual fact, the home team always managed to hit more home runs and score more runs than the less favored out-of-towners.

On occasion this, too, might evolve into a life-sized reality played out with some of the neighborhood kids. If the occasion gave the appearance that it might have to be a quick game, we would play the game between the house and barn, using the granary as our backstop and any debris that happened to be lying nearby as our bases. As time passed and our growing adolescent power made driving the ball into the side of the house a common possibility, putting the house's windows into serious jeopardy not to mention the siding, we were required to use a whiffle-ball if we wished to play there. This not only limited our display of power but also reduced our fielding percentages due to its "whiffling." Such limitations often resulted in our moving the game from the home park to the county park which bordered our farm on the far east-end. There, an actual ball field, boasting a backstop and real bases but lacking outfield fences, quenched our thirst for realism. While a large dinner bell mounted in our back yard would eventually summon everyone home, sometimes our intensity or our desire to finish an inning would delay our return which would inevitably result in a stern, albeit not too threatening, lecture about it not happening again, "or else...."

Looking back, there never seemed to be enough light in the day for us to check-off all our play options, but at the time, we never considered not having a tomorrow on which to resume them. Unfortunately, the passing of time tends to drench one's face in the cold water realities of responsible adulthood and the inevitable waning of strength and health which all serve as reminders that the child in us might be slipping away as surely as the batteries in a well used video game or the value of a coin in a slot machine. I admit that Scripture confuses me a bit when, on the one hand, it admonishes us to lay aside our childish things and thinking, and then, but a short time later, it promises to hand over the keys of the kingdom to those with child-like attributes. What this says to me is that we should never lose our ability to play. Maybe that is why I find myself feeling sorry for those who are able but unwilling to play either because they have forgotten how or no longer feel they can.

FOUR

Icicles

The goal of life is living in agreement with nature.

-Zeno

OUR HOME WAS SMALL OF frame. While a overly zealous realtor might be tempted to list it as a two-story three bedroom home with three half-baths and a full basement, it would more accurately be described as a story-and-a-half three bedroom home with portable facilities under each bed all sandwiched between an unfinished attic and an always damp and musty smelling Michigan cellar, both of which housed a wide variety of spiders and as yet unidentified creatures.

Fortunately, except for an occasional thunderstorm that would knock the power out for a day or two, our house did feature electricity and drinking water pumped from a deep well located in what formerly was considered to be our milk house, a structure attached to our house in which we kept cool the cans of milk extracted twice a day from Dad's herd of Guernsey cows. Rainwater, collected from the downspouts, flowed into a cistern located under the front porch for Mom's use on laundry day, which she religiously relegated to Monday's to-do list. But as for a bathroom featuring a tub, shower, stool, and sink, in terms of our youthful reasoning, it seemed to be a luxury enjoyed only by the rich, who just happened to be everybody in our neighborhood except us. Despite our lacking these more typical in-house amenities, somehow we managed to still get our more basic needs met.

As for a shower, it was non-existent unless running around in the rain or being chased by a sibling with a garden hose counted. And to say that we had a bath tub would be a stretch unless you might consider a galvanized vat used for washing the milking machines to suffice as one. Actually, it was not until I, along with a couple of other kids from my class, was invited for an over-night to the home of our new fourth grade teacher, Miss Peterson, who replaced Mrs. Hunter midway through the year for reasons never shared, that I could truthfully say I was exposed to a real bath tub. A bath tub large enough to enjoy without having to become a human pretzel, a tangle of arms and legs all knotted up in close proximity with the chin, which was our typical fare in the vat located in our more recently constructed milk house now attached to the barn. The new milk house was a building located approximately fifty to sixty yards from our house, and it was home to a brand new bulk tank which met the State's requirement for the modernization of Dad's milking routine. It proved to be a distance often traversed in haste and not without potential snafus. As it was, in our home, "baths" were scheduled for every Saturday, whether we boys needed one or not, if for no other reason than "the next day was the Lord's Day." Needless to say, working on a farm often required many additional encounters with "washing up with soap and water," but such less demanding occasions were relegated to the kitchen sink.

"Bath-taking" in the summertime was easier and less risky than in the winter. When Mom declared it was time for us boys to take a bath, I would head for the milk-house with a towel, if I remembered to bring one. In the summertime, as warm water filled the vat, I would disrobe and stand on the pile created by my dirty clothes to avoid the habitually cold cement milk house floor. Climbing into the vat was a task made easier only by my growing taller. Since I had games to play and things to do, loitering was not something I indulged in. Declaring myself "clean," I would be in and out in as much time as it would take me to down a piece of Mom's apple cobbler topped with ice cream. A quick once-over with the towel would suffice, and grabbing my dirty clothes, I would pause only long enough to peak out the milk-house door toward the road before streaking out. Because our road was unpaved, I knew that any cars traversing it would send up plumbs of dust (unless, of course, it was raining or had done so very recently) alerting me to stay hidden behind the door until the coast was clear. Once I had determined it to be safe, holding my clothes in front of me, just in case I might have made an error in judgment, I would make a beeline for the house, my little buns following close behind. While seldom would I ever vocalize those black-listed words that Mom had threatened to wash my mouth out with soap if she ever heard me say them, I can honestly say that one or two of them would slip out of my mouth unrestrained whenever I would drop an article of clothing en route and would have to bend over to pick it up, inadvertently mooning any casual observers, before resuming my flight to the house. Fortunately for me, Mom was not ever within earshot and was thankfully not too adept at reading lips. Years later, she would still chuckle as she confessed to having often observed such comical scenes from our kitchen window.

As you can imagine, wintertime was another story. Even though the milk-house was unheated, the bathing routine was the same except for the fact that the floor was now even colder, and cars traveling a snowy or icy road seldom if ever kicked up a plumb of anything, making the distance between the milk-house and the house even more treacherous. Not wanting to re-dress in dirty clothes when I forgot to bring clean clothes with me, required an acute ear if I wished to avoid X-rated encounters with gawking passers-by. In addition, dropping an article of clothing in the snow or losing an unlaced shoe almost guaranteed that my hair would be a frozen mass by the time I made it to the front door of the house, not to mention the fate of my other extremities.

As for the other necessity, our outhouse shared its responsibility with the backside of a bush or tree or just about any other out-of-sight location during the day, especially for the four males in our family. The original outhouse was an enclosed structure featuring a two-by-six foot bench with two holes cut into it. For comfort's sake, someone had taken the time to bevel the holes and locate them far enough from each other that should a circumstance require it, there would be adequate space to accommodate two users at the same time. While my backside appreciated the beveling, I was always curious as to what would necessitate the two holes since the manner and purpose for which this facility was to be used never seemed to be a proper occasion for the welcoming of guests; then again, perhaps it was one of those extra features a realtor could get some mileage out of.

Alternative portable facilities were also located in multiple strategic areas in the house to adequately serve night-time purposes. Located under each of our beds, these facilities were commonly referred to as "the pot." They were intended for night-time use only or in the event of an unexpected urgency that might prohibit someone from making it in a timely manner to the outhouse, or to one of those other out-of-sight out-of-doors locations. Usually, it fell to each of us to empty the contents of our own porcelain pot as dictated by the level of liquid or the level of Mom's olfactory tolerance, a tolerance definitely lowered by our tendency to often forget to replace the lid.

As far as some realtors might be concerned, we had central heating. But for us it merely meant that our octopus-like wood and coal burning furnace was situated in the center of our basement. When I first heard in science class that "heat rises," I was convinced that whoever had researched this had never lived in our house. In the wintertime, our unheated upstairs would rival any modern day walk-in freezer. My parents would leave the door leading to the upstairs open at night "to let some heat up," something they, too, were obviously misinformed about but stalwartly convinced that by so doing, it would warm the upstairs. Even though the evidence was there, given the fact that the furnace usually went out sometime during the night, and when the wind was blowing just right, a snow drift would find its way through the cracks around our bedroom windows, my parents were unable to justify the expense of directing heat to the upstairs. In their defense, they did make sure that each of our beds featured "winter-time" flannel sheets and two or three horse blankets that seemed, evidenced by their weight, to also include the horse. Pinned beneath this bedding, we were warm, but for all intents and purposes, immobilized. Such repressive conditions would dictate that we would have to be in dire need to use the facilities in the middle of the night before we would even consider attempting to free ourselves from the vice-like grip of our bedding and venture forth to kneel on an icy floor in order to pay our respects to the porcelain pot beneath our beds.

It was in the middle of one of those nights that I found myself having to be creative. It was not unusual for the contents of one's porcelain pot to freeze solid during those winter months, a situation that would result, to our glee, in a popsicle-like creation when emptied outside in a snow bank. I recall having decided earlier that morning after having used the porcelain pot during the night that it would be in need of empting prior to nightfall. But as usually happens with good intentions during the day of a busy child, I forgot to do so until it came to me in the pitch blackness of my room that night. As I was lying there in the dark knowing that I would not be able to hold it until morning, I recall leveraging myself out of bed and kneeling to feel for the porcelain pot. As soon as my hand located it, I remembered my unfulfilled intention, and it prompted my fear that the pot might be too full to bear additional input. I had to make a quick decision. It seemed that I had three choices: I could take a chance that the pot might not overflow; I could make my way downstairs, dress myself appropriately for the weather, trudge through the dark to an equally dark outhouse, and pry open the door, probably fighting the resistance of a snow drift that usually made its way there during the night; or I could take advantage of the crack beneath my bedroom window. The latter made more sense from a comfort standpoint. So it was that I made my decision, convinced that using the crack under the window was the best solution; after all, neither an over-flowing porcelain pot nor waking my parents would prove to be a good thing.

Needless to say, the evidence of my decision was made very clear in the morning light as the most beautiful yellow icicles hung from beneath my window sill. My mom took advantage of the occasion to passionately re-explain to me how "our sins will find us out," while Dad proceeded to instruct me how I was to use the long pole he had retrieved from the tool-shed to knock down every icicle that hung from our eaves, even if they were not the ones I had tinted. To this day I chuckle when I see my grandchildren sucking on an icicle.... I do not think there is a realtor alive who could have made this out to be anything other than what it was.

FIVE

Poncho

If you wish to travel far and fast, travel light. Take off all your envies, jealousies, unforgiveness, selfishness and fears.

-Cesare Pavese

GROWING UP, OUR FARM WAS home to all sorts of animals, some domestic and many "otherwise." With one exception the role of those considered domestics was one of function devoid of much relationship. The presence of those that teetered somewhere between the domestics and the "otherwise" often were tolerated because of their ability to eliminate those deemed more feral and thus less desirable. Case in point, take our cats, for instance.

Though typically domesticated by nurturing, nature's original intent was not wasted on our farm. An unwritten contract permitted their residency on the farm in exchange for their vigilance in safeguarding the barn and the outbuildings against the relentless invasions of mice, rats and birds that for some reason saw fit to become squatters just about anywhere they wanted. Because of their sheer numbers and their frequent unexplained appearances and disappearances, it was futile, if not impossible, to try to befriend our cats much less name them. It seemed as if the arrival of new litters were a weekly occurrence while survival of only the fittest weaned their numbers at an almost equal pace. Failure to recall a particular marking might indicate the presence of a stray that somehow found its way to the drinking cup that we filled twice a day with warm milk fresh from the source, but because time and effort were always at a premium on the farm, culling them made little sense, especially when we could not always be sure which ones were actually ours. By nature all cats are territorial, and "barn-cats" are no exception. Any invasion of their turf automatically guaranteed a hissing-fit intended to give the intruder fair warning that they fully intend to fight rather than take flight. Such vocalizing never fazed my dad, but we kids took their warning seriously and always kept our distance no matter how young and cute they happened to be.

Meanwhile, my brothers and I did attempt to name most of our more domestic animals at one point or another, indicating the esteem with which we held them; however, the real value of the cows, chickens, sheep, and our one horse was based solely on their ability to contribute to life on the farm. These animals faithfully fulfilled their specific functions until such time as their contributions no longer justified the amount of feed they consumed, or their health no longer justified the continued expense of a veterinarian at which time typically their tenure would be celebrated on our dinner table (with the exception of the horse, of course). Thus it was, to consider any of the animals on our farm as pets would require stretching that relational definition beyond the point of Webster's intent.

However, there was one exception to the rule. It was our dog Poncho, a domestic who served not only a functional role but a relational one as well. He was as adept at bringing in the cows, once directed to "Fetch 'em," and scaring up wild game once directed to "Sic 'em," as he was friendly, protective, and unconditionally loyal.

Because ours was a home in which the electrical outlets never held hands with a TV, our windows and doors to the outside world were adult conversations, sermons, books, discarded *National Geographics, Weekly Readers,* and radio. This being the case, for entertainment we would often listen to such radio programs as *The Shadow, The Lone Ranger, Our Miss Brooks, Sergeant Preston of the Yukon,* and others, one of our favorites being *The Cisco Kid.* While I am unclear as to how our dog was actually dubbed Poncho, my assumption is that we named him after the radio namesake, Poncho, who was scripted as the Cisco Kid's faithful companion and sidekick. A cross between a collie and shepherd, our Poncho was not only a great pet, always willing and ready to work and play, but he was also a great confidant. His on-demand availability and undivided attention I especially appreciated when things were not going particularly well with my friends or family members, and his willingness to hold these secret revelations in strictest confidence ranked him right up there among my best friends. I recall that he had a peculiar way of pausing his habitual panting, then cocking his head and slightly lifting his ears at precisely those moments when I sensed that he did not quite understand what I was sharing with him, as if to say "Tell me more" or "Please clarify that." Then after a rather lengthy reiteration, he would cock his head in the other direction, roll his tongue over the tip of his nose, and resume his panting while looking straight at me as if to say, "Oh, now I get it, please continue."

Tirelessly, he always seemed to be in the right place at the right time every time, and even when he would take a momentary respite in the sun or in the shade of the old walnut tree, his ears would be poised as if to catch the slightest hint that his services might be needed. Life was good for Poncho, and he returned the favor, that is until that one day which changed things forever.

It was mid-October, and this particular morning dawned frosty, cool, and crisp, hinting that the impending winter was every bit as guaranteed as the outcome of a professional wrestling match. Over breakfast, Dad announced that in order to make room for this year's crop, we would be chopping the last of the corn stalks piled next to the barn. The stalks were there as a result of an elaborate series of events, the onset of which would begin sometime in mid-to-late September when Dad declared that the corn in the field was "ready" for husking, a determination he would make after pressing his fingernails into the kernels of randomly selected ears and being unable to extract any "milk" from them. When such was the case, my two brothers and I, along with my dad and any of my uncles who might be available and wanting to make a few extra dollars, would head into the corn fields wielding corn knives.

Once there, the first thing we would do is form a corn shock which required us to take one or two uncut corn stalks from adjacent rows, bend them over each other and weave them together to form an interlocking crisscross framework. Then using our corn knifes which featured a wooden handle about a foot-and-a-half long attached to a sharpened curved steel blade, we would cut the corn stalks located around this newly formed structure about two-to-four inches from their root and lean them against the framework. When the adults involved would declare that we had, in fact, made the corn shock large enough, using a piece of binder twine, we would then encircle and tie the tops together, a process that would be repeated over and over until all the corn earmarked for husking would be successfully shocked and bound. This entire process usually took a week or two, and upon completion it would leave the field looking somewhat like an Indian village replete with strategically aligned teepees.

With this part of the process now having been completed, and the stalks in the shocks having had some additional time to dry, the husking would begin. Locating and cutting those stalks used to form the base of the shock, we would push the entire structure over unto the ground, and releasing the binder twine, we would then kneel on the ground or sit on wooden crates facing each other from opposite sides and begin the husking process as well as the rambling conversations that were always so much a part of the process.

Husking is an art all of its own. The more experienced huskers would be seen using their favorite husking pin, which typically featured a looped leather strap attached to a small knife-like metal bar honed and slightly curled at one end, looking like the beak of a field hawk. The leather loops accommodated the fingers, which when placed through them and pushed down to the base of the fingers at the palm of the hand, readied one to begin stripping away the husks using the curled end of the pin. Once stripped of its husks, the golden symmetrically shaped ear would be snapped off and tossed into a pile on the ground to be picked up later.

With the exception of Sundays and depending on the weather, husking could be a daily event for the better part of three to four weeks. Since such days would often span the time between the early morning and early evening milking, Mom would always pack a lunch and a thermos or two of coffee, the smells of which I now reason might be why I am so attracted to the aroma of coffee even to this day, having somehow come to associate it with a much earned respite. The sandwiches Mom would pack, however, usually lacked something. Having been wrapped in wax paper and placed in a lunch pail the night before, those sandwiches could be more than a bit dry by the time lunch-time was finally declared. While baked bean sandwiches seemed to retain some of their original moisture better than our cow tongue, cheese, or peanut butter sandwiches, they too could become as dry as the corn we were husking, and yet we always did our best to make them disappear because as my Uncle Cornell would have us believe, "If we don't eat everything today, we'll likely get less tomorrow!" which we feared might include the cookies and pieces of cake or pie Mom often packed as a special treat to compensate for what might be lacking in the main course. As it was, the mice often had a field day with our sandwiches but never our compensations.

Once it was determined that a sufficient number of piles of corn had been husked to fill the back of Dad's pickup truck, or that there existed an imminent threat of rain or snow, Dad would drive the truck to the field. There we would load the piles of corn by hand and then drive the load back to the farm for storage in the corn crib where we would unload it in the same effective but inefficient manner in which we had loaded it.

Since nothing was ever wasted on our farm, the earless corn stalks, too, after having been re-bundled, eventually found their way to the side of our barn, where they would be laid to rest on a criss-cross frame of old railroad ties or discarded telephone poles. This frame not only invited the circulation of air, while discouraging the curse of mold and mildew that would render the stalks useless as sustenance for Dad's herd through the winter months, but it also served as an invitation for varmints of every ilk seeking a safe and warm respite from the cold. As needed, these stalks would be chopped and blown onto the barn floor and later fed to the cows; what the cows failed to eat eventually wound up as bedding.

Each time we would do a chopping, the stack would grow smaller, until one day only a handful of bundles would remain. It was at such times that our eager anticipation would begin to peak as we awaited the revelation of the "something" that might have made its home under the stack this year. Historically, a rat or two, a skunk, a woodchuck, a raccoon, a possum, a weasel, or even an occasional snake would find refuge there from the weather and their foes further up the food chain. Each year that "something" seemed determined to remain under the very last bundle until the very last moment when with a great deal of fearful anticipation, which we were careful to camouflage by an equally great deal of bravado, one of us, wielding an extra long handled pitchfork, would carefully lift the bundle from the frame.

Poncho was never a stranger to such unveilings. His barking, snorting, digging, and jumping around evidenced his adrenaline-fueled instincts, and when once that final bundle would be lifted, revealing whatever it was that may have found refuge there, it was destined to do battle with Poncho.

I recall this one particular day in mid-November that the lifting of the last bundle revealed the presence of a large raccoon. It wrestled for a minute or two with Poncho, amid yelps and hisses, before making a beeline for the old brooder coup in the orchard, with Poncho nipping at its heels in hot pursuit. The raccoon eventually managed to find safe harbor under the coup and between the large telephone-like poles on which the coop had been constructed. Such construction was intended to permit mobility should the coup need to be moved, as well as to prohibit the floor of the coop from making direct contact with the ground in an effort to discourage dry rot and to avoid it becoming an open invitation for all the local termites to come and feast. The space between the coup and the ground, however, was just too small to give Poncho room to continue his pursuit, but it did not prohibit him from going wild with his barking and frantic pawing of the ground. Meanwhile, my older brother decided to retrieve Dad's 16-gauge shotgun from the old milk house which, as mentioned before, no longer served its original intent. A casualty of new regulations, it had fallen into disuse except to provide shelter for some of Dad's tools, his gun, and also the well that to this day still supplies water to both the house and the barn.

Grabbing the gun and a handful of shells from one of its dusty and cobweb-laden shelves, my brother headed back to the coop, intent on flushing the coon out into the open so as to give Poncho another go at it. Lying down on the ground next to Poncho to get a better view of the coon's location, my brother took dead aim. Meanwhile, Poncho, having been brushed aside to make room for my brother, went around to the other side, perhaps in anticipation of the coon's extradition, a fact my brother became aware of a split second after his finger had squeezed the trigger. I do not recall if the shot impacted the coon or not, but it caught Poncho full in the face, pummeling his snout with a blizzard of BBs. Poncho's shrill mournful yelping and the rivers of blood streaming from his nose as he fled the scene are still etched in my memory.

For weeks, Poncho laid in the dark beneath the steps of our woodshed, inconsolably whimpering and instinctually doing what animals do to nurse their wounds. Because our family's meager finances were reserved only for the cows that produced, Poncho's fate would be self-determined. I hated my brother for killing "my best friend." Even though Poncho eventually healed and lived for a couple of years after that fateful day, he was never the same again. His instinctive fire had been snuffed out, draining him of his desire to participate in life as he once did. Now merely a shell of his former existence, he cowered behind his sad eyes and drooping ears. Not yet familiar with or having experienced the hard reality of impermanence, until he disappeared one day never to return, I innocently prayed for things to be as they once were.

Even though I knew my brother felt terrible, my unforgiving silence sentenced him to feel my resentment and pain as well. No doubt, even to this day whenever I think on these things, I regret not only the loss of the innocent companionship Poncho afforded me so many years ago, but equally so my long-lasting, unforgiving silent condemnation of my brother who has since that day suffered so many losses of his own. Now if "living happily ever after" is the type of optimistic attitude that has yet to come up against in-laws, kids, carpools or siblings who kill your "best friend," perhaps the best we can do to ensure a measure of it is to be forgiving not only of others but of ourselves as well. After all, this might be one of the few things that separate the domestics from the feral, the functional from the relational, and the human from the divine.

SIX

Grandpa

Grandfathers are just antique little boys.
-Unknown

AS WE AGE BEYOND MERELY the physical, it becomes ever more apparent, at least to those closest to us, that our mental disposition over the years either can become more crotchety or more *que sera sera*. This becomes evident by our growing tendency to either kick against the pricks or to go with the flow. I would like to think that the decision for evolving one way or the other is something one can choose, perhaps in the same way that one might opt for wearing a particular pair of socks over another. Doubtless, there are those who would deem this thinking to be far too simple an explanation for a far too complicated evolution, but it serves my purpose.

There are some who might argue that life circumstances cause as well as legitimize our attitudes, but while they may be capable of making a pretty good case that unhappy people are the result of their unhappy experiences and vice versa, perhaps they have forgotten that a little rain falls and a little sun shines in everyone's life. What is to be done with the mantra "As one thinks, so is he?" Do we actually get what we cultivate in our thoughts? Like seeds, do our thoughts take root in our experiences? Would not one's observations and personal experiences naturally argue against the idea that similar experiences of necessity ensure similar reactions, and more to the point, engender similar attitudes? Granted, there are those who feel strongly that the deck is always stacked against them, especially when that stacking pertains to the negative, but might those who feel this way have merely lost sight of the fact that often over time many things once thought to have been a curse have proved to be a blessing; what earlier seemed meant for evil was later deemed for good—or put another way, "Can we really know enough to be a pessimist?"

There are others who claim that one's outlook on life might be the result of a singular life changing event. "Seeing the light" or "Hitting the bottom" are a couple of the phrases often used to describe such life changing experiences. At first blush there might appear to be some legitimacy in this thinking, but a case can be made that perhaps such reasoning makes as much sense as concluding that because someone once spoke harshly to you, it proves that you must not be a good person. While holding unto the singular life changing experience theory might make more sense if we were to weigh in on the severity of such an experience, it seems that an even more logical argument could be made that when such an experience is added to one's other experiences, perhaps at some point a critical mass is reached. This being the case, then one's disposition may merely be the result of a mathematical tally- a score keeping, which, when weighed in on attitudinal scales, could be used as a justification for its tipping one way or the other. Then again, perhaps all such considerations merely boil down to yet another "chicken or egg" dilemma: Does our attitude determine our life's experiences, or do our life experiences determine our attitude?

All that being said, maybe there is little or no merit in determining the cause or sequence of events that encourage one disposition over the other, but suffice it to say, my paternal grandfather, by general consensus, was crotchety. Few there were who spoke of him, but those who did described him as a shriveled, sober, and somber man whose joy and laughter, if ever he had them, had long ago trickled out of him. The winter of his discontent seemed to also include spring, summer, and fall. While I do not think his disposition was such that people were waiting to gleefully dance on his grave, I doubted seriously that many would mourn his passing either. Those who gave him a second thought probably figured he would just fade away, and the space he left where once he was would hastily follow suit.

Early on, I recall my mom admonishing my brothers and me to never cross Grandpa as he had a long memory, evidenced by the number of people with whom he was no longer on speaking terms. Dad would advise us to keep our distance which meant to avoid "bothering" him, monkeying around with his things, or treading recklessly in his garden. As a youngster I was not privy to Grandpa's history or personal experiences, nor did I care to be, but I do recall feeling somewhat sorry for him because the bits and pieces of my experiences with him formed quite a different mosaic than that viewed by most. After all, growing up a stone's throw down the road from where he and Grandma lived, I certainly felt I knew him better than most.

Many there were who thought Grandpa was just born grumpy, giving no consideration to the fact that maybe they just misunderstood him; maybe his past had caught up with him, or perhaps he was merely a victim of one or more of his own life changing experiences. Maybe his thoughts were such that his experiences followed suit, or maybe his experiences were what caused him to think and act as he did. Then again, maybe his typical unemotional, often silent-as-ice, demeanor had no rhyme or reason at all. It was just his way. Be that as it may, I had a hard time resonating with the prevailing general consensus, that is, until that day–a day on which I would be forced to come face-to-face with the reality of a "life changing" experience of my own.

But before getting to that, I want you to get to know a little more about my relationship with my grandpa. Growing up, I learned that most of the neighborhood kids were scared to death of him; I reasoned that was because he always looked angry. His wrinkles had carved a permanent frown, doing little to dispel what others saw as his countenance. While most of the kids he encountered could relate real or imagined occasions when he "barked" at them, in his defense, that is something adults did back then when kids were not minding their manners or P's and Q's, and it seemed that Grandpa might have co-authored the book on both of these. While sensing that his "bark" was always worse than his "bite," but being careful not to let on to my friends that my opinion of him differed from theirs, I was secretly glad for the affinity he and I seemed to have. Even to this day, I credit Grandpa with a number of things that have helped to impact my own life. Case in point, I credit him with my sustained love for fishing.

During many of those lazy days of summer when the farm did not demand my immediate presence, often when he and one or two fishing buddies would head to the local pier because they had heard the perch were biting, he would take me with them. What ten year old would not feel that sitting on a five gallon plastic bucket fishing alongside a couple of older guys was not just about the most adult thing a kid could do? Looking back, I am convinced it was my patience that first caught Grandpa's attention, and perhaps because of it I was the "elected one" among all of his grandchildren to be invited to fish with him. Validated by adult conversations I would overhear from time to time, my patience had already been judged to exceed that of most ten year olds. Because Grandpa always moved so slowly, I figured he was all about patience, and he certainly deserves credit for further nurturing and honing mine.

For example, I was smart enough to figure out that if I wished to continue going with him on these fishing expeditions, I would need to reel in some of that more natural boyhood behavior including some physical restraints. One such restraint has proved to result in a well trained bladder that, to this day at least, sets me apart from most of my peers. Early on, I learned what it meant to "go before you went" if for no other reason than the portable structures near the pier were nowhere near the pier, and on those particularly hot and humid days, despite their distance from the pier, the smells emanating from them rivaled the stench of week-old fish entrails baking in the open sun. Interesting how learning to hold back such a natural urge while fishing for hours on end seems so much easier then than now. Needless to say, knowing this has deepened my appreciation for Grandpa's ability to manage such things. Perhaps, what ability I still have in this arena is as much a factor of heredity as it is of environment; this being the case, my grandpa deserves a major portion of the credit.

Long before he ever purchased fiberglass fishing gear with open faced reels, all of Grandpa's poles were of the bamboo cane variety with fishing line wound around their tips. Being far too long for interior transport, these cane poles had to be tied to the exterior door handles of Grandpa's four-door car which he did using binder twine from the farm. This surely alerted everyone in town, who took the time to glance in our direction, we were going fishing. Grandpa always made sure there was an ample supply of black nylon fishing line, sinkers, fish hooks and bobbers in anticipation of losing some of them on snags, often referred to during the retelling of fish sagas as "the big ones that got away."

Turning these poles in your hand one way or the other was a very inefficient but effective retrieval or letting out of the line procedure. Often such rigging and procedures afforded me additional opportunities to practice patience, especially when my line would become tangled, which it often did. On such occasions, as dictated by Grandpa, I would be careful to place my pole on the pier so others would not trip over it and then commence to untangle the spaghetti-like mess held captive by its two hooks, sinker, and bobber, trying as best I could to accomplish this feat with all the patience and non-verbal grumbling of the Biblical character Job. As I labored in silent disgust, I could feel Grandpa's penetrating eyes on me as if he were almost enjoying my dilemma. Sucking on his pipe, which usually was in need of a reload or re-light, something he would busy himself doing whenever the fish had decided not to bother him, Grandpa would mutter between clinched teeth clamped tightly on the pipe's stem, "You can't catch fish if your line's not in the water." He would then chuckle under his breath as if he had just told one of his favorite fishing jokes. Not wanting to upset him or jeopardize any future chances I might have of accompanying him, I would hide my true feelings beneath a pasted on smile and forced chuckle, pretending that what I was doing was exactly what I wanted to be doing and that I was even enjoying it. While some pier-walkers might have considered it inconsiderate that my grandpa would not help a little kid as he struggled to straighten his line, I admit that I found a great deal of satisfaction whenever I ultimately undid the knotting, which I always was able to do as long as time was not a factor. As the years passed, I continue to find personal satisfaction in independently resolving issues using the same self-determined resolution and persistence, all the while guarding the expressions of my true feelings when things do not quite go as I would like.

Every once in a while, yet far too often, my carelessness would result in breaking the tip off one of Grandpa's poles. If this happened on the pier, I was in deep trouble. At such times whenever the tip became mysteriously detached, I knew that my fishing was finished for the day. Despite my pleading offers to try to fix it, Grandpa would hear nothing of it. As Dad said, you do not monkey with Grandpa's stuff and that, I concluded all on my own, included his fishing poles. So I would either be left to nap on the pier, to enviously watch other fisherman effortlessly angle with their more modern equipment, or to gawk with unexplained pre-adolescent interest at some of the girls traversing the pier in bathing suits that looked so much different from the ones my mom would wear. Relief would come when Grandpa would finally announce that we ought to be "calling it a day." Interestingly, Grandpa never reprimanded me for my carelessness when it came to his fishing poles, but his silence was deafening. Under such circumstances, there was one thing I could always count on the next time I would join the guys fishing, and that is my pole would be a bit shorter. It was apparent Grandpa had removed the broken tip and rewrapped the fishing line on what remained. I recall with particular embarrassment the day when my pole no longer needed to hang out on the door handles but rather could be transported inside Grandpa's car. I was convinced, but careful never to verbalize it, that such re-riggings put me at a great disadvantage, setting me apart from the others whose longer poles allowed them to fish a wider radius and with more sensitivity. Perhaps this was my punishment. But then again on the plus side, perhaps Grandpa can be credited with the fact that I now sport the most up-to-date fishing equipment and have cultivated a deeper appreciation for certain types of swimming apparel.

My life with him did not afford much physical proximity beyond those fishing expeditions or helping him put together an occasional jigsaw puzzle when the snow and cold spelled the end of our trips to the pier. Our time together was seldom interrupted with conversation, but on those rare occasions when Grandpa would actually make an attempt at conversation, it was often instructional in nature, salted and peppered with old sayings and adages pertaining to the task at hand. While I did not fully understand them at the time, years later these same old sayings and adages somehow managed to find their way into many a conversation I have had with my own children and grandchildren. In defense of Grandpa, he was always busy raising his rabbits, working in his garden, smoking his pipe, and "fussing" (Grandma's term for what he did that didn't matter) to involve himself in the real work of human contact. For all intents and purposes, Grandpa was a loner, and such living within himself seemed to be okay with him and everybody else, me included... until that day.

I recall that morning dawned as any other, except that the sun seemed to have yoked the sky a bit earlier than usual, maybe because I was feeling a certain lightness and relief. Despite the fact that I was to stand before my teachers and peers, along with their parents and relatives, later that evening to deliver a high school graduation speech on behalf of my class, I was too excited to angst over the details. Having written and practiced my speech to the point of nausea, combined with all the adolescent cockiness of a graduating senior with a firm grip on the tail of the world, I was confident all would go well. Having weeks ago completed my classwork and exams, I anticipated coasting into the events of the evening without a worry or fret.

I was sitting at the breakfast table that morning downing Mom's daily regimen of lumpy oatmeal and toast when my reverie was broken by the ringing of our party-line phone. It was our ring; one long and two short. Mom answered. It was Grandma, wondering if we had seen Grandpa. Occasionally, but not as often as he once used to, Grandpa would mosey up the path through the field to visit Dad in the barn or "just walk around." I do not particularly recall that such trips had any utilitarian intentions or benefits, and I never considered Grandpa to be the nostalgic type nor one who would walk for the sake of exercise or conversation, so why he would occasionally make these little excursions to the farm that he once owned was always a bit beyond me.

As Mom hung up the phone, she asked me to check in the barn while she headed for the upstairs windows where her eyes could better comb the fields. Having done as I was instructed, to no avail, I found that Mom was also unsuccessful in eyeing Grandpa. At that point she called Grandma to report the results of our reconnaissance. Meanwhile, with breakfast finished, I took to tackling the lawn. While it was the one and only chore I was assigned for the day, it would prove to be a difficult one nonetheless, made more so by having to use the same ancient reel push mower with dull blades that my younger brother and I had used years ago. The fact that the grass had not seen a mower for over two weeks did not help matters. Mom, meanwhile, returned to her canning, a task she took quite seriously and one I learned years later had been prompted by the life thrust upon her as a child growing up during the Depression.

The better part of half an hour had passed when Mom called to me from the front porch, asking if I would go down and look for Grandpa in his "rabbit barn." Grandma maintained that even though Grandpa had sold the "big" farm to my dad some years earlier, Grandpa's transition to what she referred to as the "city-life" was difficult for him; so as it was, Grandma permitted him to construct a small barn on the one acre they had retained in the sale. Despite only being of the size that could accommodate some caged rabbits, a workbench, some odds and ends, and a few bales of hay stored in the upstairs loft, it apparently was enough to relieve Grandpa of his concern for being labeled a "city-slicker."

Apparently, Grandma felt that Grandpa would just show up after a while, but when half an hour had passed and there was still no sign of him, and after having on numerous occasions unsuccessfully called out to him, something Grandma would typically accredit to what she disgustingly referred to as his "hearing limitations," and being unable to maneuver well herself, she finally opted for having one of us more agile boys take on the task of physically checking out Grandpa's barn. Looking back, I am not sure how I did it, but somehow I was successful in convincing my mom to send my older brother, who had just come up to the house after having completed his morning chores, reasoning that I had a little more mowing to do to finish up and that I needed some time to go over my speech. Unconvinced that the reason Mom chose to send him in my stead was legitimate, and muttering under his breath how he would get even, eventually, though begrudgingly, my brother ambled through the field leading to Grandpa's barn. Meanwhile, I hurried to complete my lawn mowing task and after finishing up, I stored the mower in the tool shed and headed for the house. I recall sitting at the kitchen table sipping a lemonade Mom had poured for me, feeling only slightly guilty that I had duped her into sending my brother in my stead. Having positioned myself to watch from the kitchen window any goings on at Grandpa's house, my mom and I observed my brother walking around Grandpa's yard and then walking into his barn, only to emerge minutes later and casually walk into Grandma's house. I assumed we would soon hear from Grandma that my brother had been successful in locating Grandpa, but moments later I watched as my brother left the house and re-entered the barn. This time he remained there a bit longer than before, and what occurred next seemed so surreal that it appeared to happen in slow motion rather than in the allegro staccato in which it actually occurred.

The door of Grandpa's barn figuratively flew off its hinges as my brother burst through it, emanating the kind of blood curdling screams I am still convinced are utterly uncharacteristic of the human repertoire. As he fled the barn, I hurriedly called to Mom, who had looked away for a minute to attend her canner, and together we watched as my brother raced to the clothesline pole that functionally adorned Grandma's backyard, and clinging to it as if he might somehow find some solace there, he slid to the ground like an unhurried fireman and melted into a sobbing heap of broken humanity.

Even though the chronology of the events leading up to what we witnessed, as well as those that followed, have blurred over time, any attempt to recapture them here would serve no useful purpose. The reality was painfully plain and simple: Grandpa had hanged himself in the loft of his barn. On the day that I would launch my future, Grandpa decided that his was no longer worth his effort. I recall delivering my speech that night entitled, "The Precious Gift of Life," but to this day I am not sure how much of what I had rehearsed actually got said. While I do recall those in attendance expressing polite congratulations blended with their more hushed sympathies, I also remember thinking that perhaps under the circumstances, it made little difference if either were sincere.

SEVEN

The Outhouse

Sooner or later, everyone stops smoking.
-Unknown

SOME MIGHT PASS IT OFF as just a boyhood curiosity spurred by the commercial ads that portrayed smokers as somehow being a cut above the average guy. After all, the *Marlboro* man certainly was not going to allow sand to be kicked in his face by some beach bully. But while I was on occasion able to find and read a comic book, our family never saw fit to own a TV. My maternal grandmother referred to TV as "the work of the devil," and my mom was convinced that watching TV not only resulted in "idle hands," it also resulted in "idle minds." Fortunately, my paternal grandparents did own a TV and obviously enjoyed their idleness from time to time. But looking back, I would certainly rule out TV as having played a major role in my decision at the age of eleven, in the year of our Lord 1957, to take up the fine art of smoking.

To be honest I think it might have been more likely that my uncles planted and nourished this idea in my head. What with their cigarette packs rolled up in the sleeves of their t-shirts, exposing their farmer-tanned and muscled arms, both by-products of the demands placed upon them, they looked so cool posed against the backdrop of their fast cars and rosy cheeked girlfriends... looking so much better than that ruddy faced cowboy with his horse. Besides, what eleven-year old does not want to look cool, especially in front of girls? Because my uncles' rituals of inhalations and exhalations always took place well out of sight of my maternal grandmother, I concluded that by using some discretion, I would also be able to partake without experiencing the condemnation of those closest to me.

As it was, when I finally made up my mind to give it a try, I decided I needed an accomplice. After all, I thought, what good would it be to smoke if no one besides me could confirm my brave and manly effort? I found one! He was a next door neighbor kid, a year younger than me and two grades behind me in school. I considered him my summer friend because once the school year began, he fell into the category of "being a baby" in the presence of my classmates. He did not seem to mind, and even though I would feel a tinge of guilt from time to time for the way I treated him around my peers, I was convinced that subjecting myself to the ridicule of my classmates was too big a price to pay for making public our seasonal friendship.

Having convinced him that this would be good for his reputation at school, together we strategized a plan. Since no one in either of our immediate families smoked, we lit upon the idea of searching the shoulders of the roadways in our neighborhood for butts thoughtlessly tossed from the car windows of passers-by. Since all of the roads around our neighborhood were of the gravel and dirt sort, we considered the entire roadway a shoulder worthy of our search. They were not to be just any old butts. They needed to be long, in good condition, and definitely free of lipstick impressions. The "good ones" we collected and placed in a cigar box that had temporarily been relieved of its former contents, namely my cherished baseball cards. Our consensus was that since the box already smelled of cigars, it would certainly camouflage any odor that might alert someone as to its present contents.

We also decided to commit our little indiscretion in the dark of night, convinced it would better our odds at not getting caught. Grandpa always used to say that "not much good happens after dark," but we opted to risk it anyway. While it took a bit of convincing on my part, we decided that the best location for such an activity would be our family's outhouse, a structure no one, including our neighbors, was particularly proud of, but since we had no such indoor facility, it served a very useful purpose for our family. Since the porcelain pot located under each of our beds served our evening needs for relief, it reduced, if not eliminated, the need for one to travel out-of-doors after dark, thus leaving the outhouse virtually vacant until morning. We figured that by morning any smoke residue that might linger certainly would have had time to evaporate into the crisp morning air or at least blend into the air that usually identified this location as a fully functioning facility.

The night we selected for our coming-out was enhanced by another layer of darkness, the work of an impending storm. A strong west wind accompanied by rain pelting the structure's tin roof boosted our confidence that these conditions would all but guarantee that we would not be interrupted. Despite being touted as a two-holer, our outhouse was so small that we had to cram ourselves inside this pitch black structure. We only used a flashlight to situate ourselves and to reveal the contents of our cigar box. With a great deal of care, we each reached into the box and selected one of the very best remains from among the corpses we had collected.

It was then that my accomplice announced that he had changed his mind and really did not want to smoke, but he would stay and watch me. I do not recall his excuse, but it did not really matter. His opting out left him free to be the lookout, just in case someone, choosing to brave the elements of the evening, would decide to make one last visit before settling in for the night. Reaching for the match box I had earlier smuggled in and hidden in the rafters, I removed a match and then flipped off the flashlight fearing that the longer it remained on, the more likely someone would notice. Knowing that my accomplice had assumed a position that allowed him to peer out the door now being held slightly ajar, I placed the remains of my selected cigarette between my lips. As I struck the match along the cement floor, it instantly burst into flame. Bringing the flame to the end of the cigarette, I noticed that my hands were shaking as I inhaled a deep breath, drawing the flame into its tip.

To this day, I can still remember the searing pain in my throat as the flame all too quickly advanced from the stunted end to the filter. I quickly tossed the remains of the now charred cigarette filter down one of the holes. Only later did I conclude that perhaps the initial user of this cigarette actually knew what he was doing when he chose to discard it. As the pain in my throat commenced, my coughing and the smoke caused me to sneeze; I knew that I was not up for trying another selection any time soon. Now in utter darkness, I felt for the box that contained our initial collection, and finding it, I emptied what remained of its contents into one of the holes.

Taking the box of matches and the cigar box, now emptied of our treasure trove of discarded cigarette butts, we hurriedly left the outhouse. In hopes of eliminating even the slightest possibility of detection, we paused long enough to fan the door a couple of times. And on the spur of the moment and for insurance purposes, we also agreed to leave the door slightly ajar, something my parents frowned on, as doing so would occasionally invite a creature of the night to seek safe harbor there and scare the wits out of those who might opt for a jaunt in the midnight air to use the outdoor facility rather than take advantage of their porcelain alternative. Reminding each other of our pact not to reveal any of this to our parents, we headed back to our respective homes in total darkness.

I recall lying in bed later that night, wondering if I had proven anything to myself or to my accomplice. Would he see what I had done as something cool or not? It was not long before the tell-tale heart of fear began creeping into my consciousness, and with it came the eerie feeling that what I had done might still be found out. I could only rid myself of this gnawing sense of unsettledness by deciding to get up early in the morning just in case there might be some lingering tell-tale odors left in the wake of our experiment even though I had not thought through what I would do if there were. Such were the thoughts that kept me tossing and turning most of the night.

Rising earlier than normal the next morning, I shunned the porcelain pot in lieu of heading out to the outhouse to allay my nocturnal fears. What greeted me there was worse than any smell that might have lingered. What greeted me there was my worst nightmare. I discovered a scientific fact that heretofore had never been covered in any of my science classes. Cigarette butts float! Peering down the hole, I witnessed a virtual regatta of partially submerged u-boats floating on a calm sea of brown liquid. My mind raced. My arms were not long enough to reach down the hole and gather them up. I could not think of anything that I could use to reach them. I knew it would be a race against time. With cows to milk, my dad would be up and using this outdoor facility anytime now.

As I frantically looked around for anything I could use, my eyes came to rest on the rock pile near the outhouse. Each year the point of a plow or the disc of a cultivator would encounter a field stone. My father would repair any damage to the equipment caused by hitting these rocks and then patiently unearth the rocks and toss or roll them to the fence row. There they would eventually be picked up, placed on a stone-boat, and dragged to their new home on this growing rock pile. Picking up a couple of the more manageable sized rocks and heading quickly back into the outhouse, I recall bargaining with God that should these work to obliterate my transgression, I would never again even so much as touch another cigarette, Marlboro man be dammed.

As I pummeled these large rocks down the hole with as much precision for a direct hit as any military strategist, I recall having to step back after each release so as to avoid the backsplash. As the sound of the rock hitting the water faded, I would lean forward over the hole, and peering into it, evaluate my success or lack thereof. In what seemed like an eternity, I was finally successful in clearing the battlefield of its tell-tale causalities to the point where I was at least confident no one would be the wiser. As I breathed a sigh of relief and took one last look down the hole to be doubly sure that the putrid waters were free of debris, I returned to the house and climbed back into bed, noting that I had less than ten minutes before my dad's alarm would awaken him, and he would then awaken my brothers and me so we could all head to the barn for morning milking and chores.

I do not think my parents ever surmised what went down in the outhouse that night. If they did, they never said anything to me or my brothers. The closest they may have come to any suspicion came in the late fall of that year. Each fall, just as the weather would start to turn cold and morning frosts were fast becoming routine, my dad would clean our outhouse of its contents. Using a bucket on a long pole, he would load the manure spreader and hurry to spread its contents in the fields. Whenever this task was completed, it not only kept most of our neighbors indoors with their windows down for a few days, but those who did venture out were treated to a good nasal clearing, the result of inhaling one of nature's more potent smelling salts. Despite the ribbing Dad would get from our neighbors, he was undaunted in his determination to complete the task for another year. The fall of my smoking adventure I recall overhearing my dad confess to my mom how nice it was to have "it over with" for another year, and then add, as if it were an afterthought, that he was curious as to how so many rocks wound up in the pit of the outhouse. He never asked us kids if we knew anything about it, and I am pretty sure he died not knowing the truth.

As for me, I kept my word. I have never touched a cigarette since, and I am equally proud to say that no one has ever kicked sand in my face.

EIGHT

New Year's Eve

An optimist stays up until midnight to see the New Year in. A pessimist stays up all night to make sure the old year leaves.

-Bill Vaughn

LIKE THREADS WOOFED AND WARPED in and through a fine tapestry, my fondest childhood memories were woven amid the threads of our family traditions. The celebration of most of our holidays, for example, morphed into family traditions ultimately requiring little or no inquiry or pre-planning for these special days as everyone pretty much knew what would happen when, where, and with whom, even though the "why" often remained elusive.

The celebration of New Year's Eve was one such tradition for our family. Until I reached that age when I determined it was no longer cool to do stuff with my parents, at 8:00 p.m. on the eve of each New Year, we knew that Mom and Dad would pack us three boys into the family car, and together we would make our way to the Boones, long-time family friends from Jamestown, Michigan. The Boones lived on a dead-end dirt road that Dad was convinced had settled to the bottom of the Ottawa County Road Commission's priority list when it came to snow removal and most everything else. Without exception, this would be something he would remind us of each time we would find ourselves plowing through snow or mud that seemed intent on grabbing our undercarriage, hugging our rocker panels, and kissing our chances of making good time in getting there goodbye. I surmised that it was his way of venting some frustration, as if by doing so the county might change its mind and resolve to make this particular road a higher priority.

While a case could be made that winters were a whole lot worse back then, suffice it to say, when visiting at this time of the year, we would often need to abandon our car at the three corners and await the arrival of the Boone's rusted no-name tractor to take us the rest of the way. The absence of cell phones required a pre-arranged time for the tractor to meet us, but it seemed that the arrangements always erred on the side of us having to wait for its arrival. When it would finally arrive and sputter to a halt, the five of us would climb aboard, and clinging to whatever we felt would give us some stability, we would brace ourselves for the half mile trip back to their home. It was always a trip which managed to lower our body temperature to the point that upon arrival, we would adhere ourselves to their registers until the heat emanating from them would once again reacquaint us with our extremities.

This particular evening would always seem to begin with our mothers congregating in the sewing room to "ooh" and "ah" over their most recently embroidered creations, to share techniques intended to unravel stitching dilemmas, and to consider ways to update their resurrected clothing patterns to be more in tune with the times and their changing anatomies. Once these topics were exhausted, they would then retreat to the kitchen where food preparation and crocheting consumed the rest of their evening amid discussions, not to be confused with gossip, focused on the hushed circumstances of the various families they both knew, and even those with whom they were less familiar. Just prior to the midnight hour everyone would be called to the kitchen table brimming with food items sure to guarantee the need for future alterations of clothing.

Our dads, on the other hand, would immediately gravitate to the dining room where they would engage in multiple card games of Kings-in-the-Corner, amid endless cups of coffee and "adult-only" snacks. Their card-playing battles would be interrupted only by nature's calling, the need for coffee refills, or the restocking of the snacks. Once in a while Mr. Boone would need to acquire additional cigarettes or another deck of cards because the deck they were using was judged to favor one or the other contestant. Because everything would eventually be enveloped in the hazy blue smoke emanating from both ends of Mr. Boone's Lucky Strikes, our dad, being a non-smoker, would occasionally have a coughing spell that prompted a stoppage of the game to allow him to stick his head outdoors for a breath of fresher air before coming back and resuming the game where they had left off. Their games would continue until they heard the call to come to the kitchen to get some food before joining with those of us already eating in the TV room, sprawled wherever there was space to view the advent of the New Year on the Boone's 13-inch black and white TV with its bulging screen.

As for us kids, upon our arrival and once we had thawed out from our tractor ride, my younger brother and I, along with the two Boone boys, would get back into our snowsuits, hats, and gloves, and looking every bit like a reunion of the *Michelin* men, the four of us would head outdoors. The Winter Olympic-like scheduled evening events would often include sledding, skating, snowmen and fort building, the latter often resulting in battles being fought with carefully shaped and properly packed snowballs as ammo. Wearing thicker skin back then contributed to our ability to engage in these activities until such time as we heard the call to the kitchen, or until it became so dark we could not see our hands in front of our faces, or until one of us would finally give in and admit losing sensation in one or more of his appendages. Thus it was that whenever one of us suggested that we make our way back to the house and to the warmth and food it promised, while there might have been sarcastic utterances of "baby" or "chicken" or some such uncomplimentary nomenclature, no one ever strenuously objected to the suggestion that we discontinue persevering in the out-of-doors.

On one of these outings, I recall it was a particularly bright evening, compliments of a full moon and stars in a cloudless sky. The four of us were sledding down the steepest hill on the unplowed road. In our experience sledding two-by-two—one lying atop the other—not only provided our sleds with additional speed, but such duality also afforded us, though we never verbalized it, companionship in the dark, and someone to share the burden of pulling the sled back up the hill once we had reached the bottom of it. Because we had already made numerous trips down the hill that night on our *Red Flyer* sleds, the sledding track had packed. This packing, combined with an occasional "greasing" of the runners of our sleds using a bar of soap confiscated from the Boone's bathroom earlier in the evening, not only increased our distance but also fed our insatiable desire for speed. (A few years later we would discover *WD-40,* which the Boone boys would then smuggle from their dad's workbench in the garage. It proved to be even more effective in giving us both speed and distance.)

Because it was my turn to steer the sled on this particular occasion, one of the older Boone boys lay on top of me with the flashlight. Even though it was not needed on this starry evening, I guess he carried it out of habit. We were clipping along at a goodly pace when my eye caught a movement on the right. Whatever it was, it had emerged from the ditch and had come along side, running at arm's length from us in perfect synchronization. Despite our labored breathing, the wind whipping past our covered ears, and the sound of our runners whizzing through the snow, I managed to direct my bunk-mate's attention toward our fellow traveler. "What *is* it?" I anxiously queried of him, not wanting to take my eyes off the path ahead long enough to make a determination of my own. He turned on the flashlight and pointed it in the direction of whatever it was that was keeping pace with us. The minute the beam captured whatever it was running alongside us, I risked a quick glance, long enough to eyeball a pair of beady eyes looking back at me with equal inquisitiveness. I immediately determined and declared, "It's a skunk!" at which time I veered sharply to the left, toppling both of us into the ditch while our beady-eyed friend continued on. Over time we so embellished the retelling of this encounter that even we were almost convinced it rivaled a "near death" experience.

On another occasion, in possession of one of Mr. Boone's cigarette lighters, we decided to combine some discarded cardboard boxes from the Boone's outdoor burning barrel with some lumber from a small, now nearly roofless, storage shed that had seen its better days and, as a result, had fallen into total disuse. On this particular cold and wintry windy night, it was our intent to start a fire that we could occasionally return to and warm ourselves during our outdoor games. It was even suggested that we might make some s'mores if we could locate the ingredients. The idea of a fire seemed to be such a logical and practical one at the time that we failed to take into consideration the fact that the wind might have something to say about the matter. Having started the fire in hopes that while we continued our play it would kindle itself into a blaze sizable enough to sufficiently warm all of us at the same time, we soon discovered that the fire had a mind of its own, and warming us was not a major part of its thinking. Before we knew it, fire was licking at the dry and porous lumber that once supported the walls of the dying shed, causing us to begin digging at the snow as feverishly as a hungry dog digging for a buried bone. Whisking snow onto the fire as quickly as our eight little hands would permit, we eventually were able to extinguish it. Hoping to cover our indiscretion, we used the skeletal remains of the fallen roof and other available boards to cover the ones now somewhat blackened and charred. This incident was never talked about again, leading me to conclude that we had dodged a bullet.

On yet another occasion, we hit on the idea that we could use the tractor to pull each other on our sleds up and down the road. Having ridden on the tractor from the corner that evening, Mr. Boone had parked it back in the door-less garage situated a good seventy-five yards from the house. The oldest of the Boone boys, apparently more adept at starting the tractor than actually driving it, had positioned himself on the tractor seat, looking every bit like a king poised on his throne. As the engine turned over and roared to life, thinking he had put it into reverse to back it out of the garage, he had inadvertently put it into first-gear. What once was a formidable and somewhat organized workbench quickly became less so, as pliers, wrenches, screw drivers, hammers, bolts, and nails went flying, producing a cacophony of musical tones as they struck here and there on the partially cemented floor. Fortunately for us, the evening was young, because while the others nearly spent the remainder of it sorting and replacing the tools as best they could, the older Boone boy and I worked feverishly to restore the bench to some facsimile of its former self. Unfortunately, that little indiscretion *was* uncovered because we had failed to take into consideration that the front of the tractor might also have been recognizably altered. Fortunately for my brothers and me, the penance for that shortcoming fell squarely onto the driver's shoulders a few days later.

A complete listing of New Year's Eve adventures at the Boone's could well be a book in itself, but suffice it to say, those nights would always slip away before we were able to sate our appetites for doing all the things we had planned to do, and all too soon we would find ourselves having to make the trip back home, reversing the process of our arrival. Once having been shuttled back to our car, we would typically find it not only burdened with a layer of freshly fallen snow but also in the clutches of knee deep drifts of the same, often compliments of an anonymous road crew which must have felt some compassion for those who lived on the main road. This situation would necessitate our having to brush off the snow and dig ourselves free using the two shovels Dad always carried in the trunk at this time of the year for that and related purposes. The combination of the tractor ride and the shoveling would once again bring us to the threshold of frostbite, and because it would take many more miles to warm up our car than we would have to travel, we kids would wrap ourselves in the blankets

Mom made sure were always in our car anytime we had any distance to travel during the winter months. I think she had read somewhere about a family that had frozen to death in their snowbound car and made a promise to herself that that would not be our plight if she had anything to say about it.

Upon finally arriving back home around 1:00 in the morning on New Year's Day and not nearly thawed, we would be greeted by an equally cold house, compliments of our coal and wood burning furnace that had been granted a five-hour furlough in our absence. As a very young boy, this was not a problem for me since I would often fall asleep in the car and have to be carried into the house and bedded in a semi-conscious state. But as I grew older, that first day of a new year became synonymous with having to eventually climb the stairs by myself to my unheated bedroom, and once there, in a semi-frozen state, having to burrow myself beneath those flannel sheets laden with horse blankets. My resolution to hibernate there for the rest of the winter would already be broken by 6 a.m. on New Year's Day when Dad would call us boys for morning milking and chores.

THE MIDDLE YEARS

NINE

Character #1- Clayton Erb

There is a thin line that separates laughter and pain,
comedy and tragedy, humor and hurt.

-Erma Bombeck

ANY NUMBER OF "CHARACTERS" LIVED in and around us as I was growing up. I use the word characters here out of deference to my mother. She used this word to reference anyone whose drum beat was even the least bit out of sync with what was considered to be the norm back then. I think it was her way of describing those individuals in the most affectionate way she could and still make her opinion known without having had to infract a Biblical admonition against calling anyone a "fool," "weird," or just plain "nuts!"

Clayton Erb was one of those characters. He was a bachelor by choice, I presume, although I was never quite sure until much later when my ability to discern became more focused and beneficial. He was just another in a long line of "less fortunate" folks my parents looked after. I always felt that the avenue of their friendship was a one-way street. Mom and Dad always seemed to be giving Mr. Erb milk from the milk house, a loaf of homemade bread, or apple upside-down cake from the kitchen, and now and again, vegetables from the family garden. I could not understand why he never returned the favors, nor did he ever show much appreciation for these friendly offerings. But Mom and Dad did not seem to mind. "After all, "Mom said, "it is just his way."

The rumors in the neighborhood orbiting around Mr. Erb were always grist for kletz and over-the-fence conversations. Some of those rumors were just plain weird, and others were downright scary. According to hearsay, Mr. Erb would never wash any of his dishes, leaving that particular chore to his odiferous hound "Buster" who, Mr. Erb boasted, would "lick them cleaner than Joy dish soap." As a child I would always snicker, appropriately, of course, whenever I heard Mr.Erb call or refer to his dog by name, because whenever it became quite obvious that the immediate atmosphere had been tainted by one of us boys, the ensuing question in our family would always be, "Okay, who let a buster?" Given the fact that wherever Mr. Erb's dog went he carried such an atmosphere, I concluded that, according to my mom's use of the word, at least Buster was aptly named.

Mr. Erb seldom attended church on Sunday (and never on Wednesday nights), and yet he would not lift a finger on the Sabbath "…out of respect," he said, "for those who did observe the 'Lord's Day.'" Despite his absence from church, however, he was never shy about punctuating his conversation with references to the "Good Lord" and "Jesus Christ." Scant evidence of the little connection he might have had with the church was embedded in the rumor that he was particularly taken by one of the widow ladies from the local Methodist Church Women's Guild, but when questioned about it, he shrugged it off, confessing only that he felt she possessed a goodly pair of muscles that could come in handy when it came time for the annual cleaning out of his barn and chicken coop. Those who were suspicious of this alleged affectation were not the least bit worried that the relationship would be going anywhere anytime soon.

In our neck of the woods, Mondays were the typical wash days, a tradition from which Mr. Erb did not exempt himself, with the exception, of course, that his practice included only the first Monday of each month, and then only if he deemed his clothes in need of "a good scrubbing." He also made a point to take a bath on that day as well. "No sense puttin' dirt in clean clothes," was his rationale. Such a lax regimen of personal hygiene might have explained why wherever he would go, he seemed to always be busy swatting flies or mosquitoes even when neither appeared to be bothering anyone else. Looking back, I figured that this fact alone might have been reason enough why he was sentenced to a life of bachelorhood.

Mr. Erb loved his chew and prided himself on hitting his spittoon more often than most of his beloved *Detroit Tigers* would hit a baseball. Of course, his misses would result in quite a mess until such time as he would instruct Buster to clean it up, a job which Buster seemed to relish despite the fact that it did nothing for his personality or his breath.

Mr. Erb never did hanker to electricity, his rationale being that if the "Good Lord" wanted us to use electricity, it seems He would have created it during the first six days. His shunning of the more modern conveniences did not seem to be because he lacked the resources to purchase them. Truth be known, the townspeople all concluded that Mr. Erb was a wealthy man, a rumor often promoted by the local married men who were jealously convinced if they had no wife or family, they, too, could be millionaires. By virtue of the fact that Mr. Erb seldom bought anything beyond the basic necessities, a list by his very nature shorter than most, it would lead one to conclude that he might have been able to save a lot of money if only he could have generated some sort of income. Because six days a week he did very little and the seventh day he rested, there seemed to be no visible revenue source, but because he was what people referred to as a "penny-pinching" bachelor, the general consensus was that Mr. Erb was continuing to store up "great wealth" somehow.

While I took all these stories and rumors in and even developed a few of my own, one day my opinion of him changed slightly for the better, leaving me to wonder if I might have judged him a bit too hastily if not too harshly. This new attitude came about as I began to notice that the traffic on the road of his relationship with my parents, and several others, actually did move in both directions.

I recall that day with some clarity. Mom typically described Mr. Erb's driving as "reckless," perhaps because he assumed he was the only driver entitled to the road. His arrival would be predictable. Horsing his twenty-four year old 1932 Ford Model B into our driveway, the pullets that were aimlessly pecking their way around the yard would scatter in fear for their lives. When he finally came to rest, it would be in a cloud of dust, the curse of numerous days without rain. Cutting the ignition, his "Bessy" would gasp for air before coughing up its dying breath in a cloud of smoke. Then he would slowly slide out from behind the wheel in an effort not only to avoid snagging his pants on the overly-exposed seat coils but also out of consideration for his arthritic knees.

When his feet finally assured him he was safely planted on the ground, and after issuing a command to Buster to "stay," he carefully maneuvered his way to the driver's-side passenger door. We watched as he undid the baling twine that held the back door shut, and reaching into the back seat, he retrieved what soon proved to be a fully unfeathered dead chicken.

Holding it by its feet, its body and headless neck swaying in rhythm with his unsteady gate, Mr. Erb approached the house. Mom greeted him, and after the briefest of exchanges that included his handing her the chicken and Mom's emotive but sincere appreciation for the offering, something he acknowledged with a head nod and a couple of embarrassed grunts, Mr. Erb made his departure replicating in reverse the fanfare of his arrival.

Mom cooked that chicken, and though it was a bit tough, our bigger challenge proved to be avoiding the BB's that seemed to somehow have permeated the meat. "Just chew carefully," was Mom's admonition after the first of its kind was discovered embedded in one of the thighs of the bird. Later, we found out that Mr. Erb had delivered a number of these pelleted poultries to others in the neighborhood and that we all were the beneficiaries of an unfortunate accident.

As the story goes, Mr. Erb was awakened during the night by the sound of frantic chickens emanating from the coop located but a few yards from his house. Anticipating that something was amiss in the henhouse, he fumbled for his lantern. Once it was successfully lit, he then pulled on his boots and put on his jacket over his long underwear. Calling for Buster, he grabbed his always loaded 16-gauge shotgun from behind the front door and headed out. The thought of encountering a fox in the henhouse was prominent in his thinking, for earlier that morning he had overheard another farmer complaining how a fox had ravaged his flock earlier in the week. Upon arriving at the coop, to his dismay, Mr. Erb noted that he had forgotten to close the small door that allowed the chickens to enter and exit during the day. Fearful that if he entered the main door it would allow the perpetrator to exit the smaller one, he bent over and pushed the lantern through the smaller opening. Placing the lantern carefully on the floor, he then pushed his gun through the opening and positioned himself on his haunches, half in and half out of the coup, to better survey the interior. While in such an unusual position, one of the unbuttoned corners on the flap to his long underwear shamelessly exposed Mr. Erb's buttock, a fact that Buster naturally found curious. Apparently, it was the combination of Mr. Erb's pensive concentration on the event unfolding in the coop and Buster's cold nose eventually making contact with his master's posterior that caused the gun to go off, resulting in the early demise of seven of Mr. Erb's prized layers...hence, the gift of chickens. While this act of kindness was the result of a misfortune, Mom always said, "The Lord works in mysterious ways" and I think if Mr. Erb were around today, he would have added a sincere "Amen" to that.

Even today, the retelling of this story by those who knew him and those who only had heard of him never fails to end in riotous laughter. No one seems to know whatever happened to the fox, or even if there ever was one. That detail no longer seemed to matter.

TEN

Character #2- Mrs. Bowman

We can easily forgive a child who is afraid of the dark;
the real tragedy of life is when men are afraid of the light.
-Plato

I HAD NEVER KNOWN MRS. Bowman to be anything other than a sophisticated, ancient, frail, fragile, and determined little woman. Since my parents would always address her by her proper name and not by her given one (a homage they respectfully reserved for anyone whom they felt was "well educated," moneyed, or of a station higher than their own, which they humbly determined to include everyone but those on the wrong side of the law), I was never privy to her first name. Of course, as kids, we were never allowed to address any adult, educated, moneyed, or otherwise, by their first name, so I never had reason to even be curious about what hers might be.

As far as I was concerned, she was just another in a long line of "characters" my mom would regularly look in on. Typically, Mom would visit her about once a month in the winter time, but she visited with her almost every Sunday night in the summer in lieu of attending our church's evening service. Though my younger brother and I were usually dragged along on these visits, if the truth be known, despite Mrs. Bowman's witch-like appearance and demureness, most of the time we were willing chaperons, especially in the summer time. We kids considered these diversions a welcomed alternative to having to sit still on unforgiving pews in a hot and stuffy church, forced to listen while a sage on the stage instilled platitudes that we were convinced were more oriented to alter adult behavior than the behavior of their inattentive children. Meanwhile, the children would play their parents for bribes of peppermints and *Dutch Bobblers* and would only "straighten up" when, in exasperation, their parents would pinch them and/or give them "that certain look" which would deliver, what all children seem to know intuitively to be, the "final" ultimatum: "Behave, or when we get home, you will wish you had."

Because the doors to Mrs. Bowman's home were never locked— "There's nothing here anyone would want, anyway," she would confess—on the evenings of our visits, we would just walk in with our "Hellos" preceding us. Secretly, I was always a bit anxious until I could hear Mrs. Bowman's dainty little voice whimper, "Come in." It gave me some assurance at least that we would not be stumbling upon a corpse. As it was, it seemed that no matter what time we arrived on those evenings, she would have already retired to what she referred to as her parlor. I once asked my mom why we did not have a "parlor," and she said that a parlor is what rich folks called their sitting room, and then went on to explain, by comparison, that it was sort of like our dining room. I reasoned since we had a dining room in our house but did not refer to it as a parlor or sitting room this might well be one more reason we could never be considered rich.

Rumored by the locals to have once been a mansion, Mrs. Bowman's home boasted four fully furnished bedrooms upstairs, each, at one time, referenced by the floral-designed paper pasted to its walls. However, as time passed, each pattern had faded to a dull facsimile of its original imprint, putting each room's distinction into jeopardy. The downstairs featured a kitchen, a dining room (or sitting room/parlor), a music room—Mrs. Bowman was rumored to have been a world-class pianist in her day which, because she had long slender fingers, easily convinced my mom that this was a likely possibility though she did not know for sure—and an arena-like living room leading out to a sparsely-toothed, wrap-around spindled porch, maligned with rotted and intermittently absent ceiling and flooring boards.

Once boasting state-of-the-art appliances, furniture, and wall and window coverings, the house over the years, like Mrs. Bowman herself, seemed to have grown tired, and now lacking attention, had fallen into varying degrees of disrepair, quilted with musty layers of dust and corpse-filled cobwebs long ago abandoned. In an effort to reduce the space in need of cleaning and required mobility, Mrs. Bowman had moved her bed into the parlor quite some time ago, thus confining her living space to it and the kitchen.

Apparently taking the idea of "retiring to the parlor" literally, it seemed that Mrs. Bowman would always be found there and already in bed. Looking back, I actually cannot say that I ever recall seeing her out of that room or out of bed for that matter. While I can still picture her crinkled waxen-face propped up on pillows, haloed by rivulets of flowing ebony and ivory hair, I can only presume that the rest of her body lay nestled somewhere between the blankets and always sterile-looking white sheets. If it were not for her piercing eyes, to me she looked every bit like a lot of those dead people I was occasionally allowed to sneak a peek at in the local funeral home while my parents paid their respects.

On those evenings, while my mom and Mrs. Bowman would converse in hushed tones, my younger brother and I would quietly busy ourselves at the parlor table with those items we insisted accompany us on such excursions. Typically, they would include our baseball cards, partially read *Hardy Boy* books, checked out from the monthly visiting Bookmobile, drawing paper, writing utensils, and occasionally the newest issue of the *Summer Weekly Reader,* which, outside of the *Prairie Farmer,* was the only periodical I recall my parents ever subscribing to.

What constituted my mom's and Mrs. Bowman's conversations I never knew, nor at that age did I care. I figured they were just the nonessential stuff that most adults talk about, but one thing was sure: They were fully capable of continuing their dialogues well beyond the limits of our preoccupation. So it was that whenever my brother and I would show signs of restlessness, if there were any light left in the day, we would be sent out-of-doors on "errands of necessity."

One such errand would be to check the outhouse to be sure that there was sufficient paper on the spindled roller and that the door was securely closed for the night. Another important task would be to take the porcelain chipped pail that always sat on her kitchen counter near the sink, to the artisan-fed stream that meandered along the back portion of her property some 40-50 yards from her house and carefully fill it, avoiding as much debris from getting into the pail as possible. Once accomplished, we would then return to the house and carefully pour the pail's contents into the side well attached to the wood burning stove that dominated the high-ceilinged wainscoted kitchen. By doing so, we ensured that Mrs. Bowman would have warm water available if and when she would be in need of it, Mom explained. Having accomplished this task, we would then have to go back and this time—ever more carefully—fill the pail with what would be Mrs. Bowman's drinking water for the week. Depending on the gravity of their topic, the anticipated length of their conversation yet to be had, and/or the availability of daylight, we could be sent back two or three times for "cleaner" water. Often, because mosquitoes were always a problem, not to mention the fact that we were convinced the eyes of various animals or even more scary human-like perpetrators were always upon us, haste would often trump our need to be careful not to ladle foreign substances into the pail.

Recalling one time when I felt that we had been asked once too often to rerun our errands, I somewhat sarcastically quizzed my mom as to who would do all these errands for Mrs. Bowman if it were not for us. I do not recall that Mom ever felt the need to respond to this particular query or any others of its nature asked in this manner, but later I learned that ever since the disappearance of her husband Ralph, Mrs. Bowman's only grown son would come once a month from the city to lend a hand. Few people had ever seen him, and those who claimed to have caught an occasional glimpse of him found him difficult to describe. The fact that a shroud of mystery hung over him, fit the overall mystique surrounding the Bowman clan that began with the unexplained and never resolved disappearance of Mr. Bowman himself, who one day took an axe into the woods and was never heard from again. Being the practical woman that she was, Mrs. Bowman's only lament was that her "Ralphy" had not only left her, but he had taken the good axe with him, leaving her with the one whose head would occasionally loosen its grip on the handle and become lodged in a log, causing all sorts of consternation over its retrieval.

Though the house was wired for electricity, as it grew darker out-of-doors, Mom would light the two kerosene lamps that were totally responsible for shedding the only light the house would witness again until the morning, amid assurances to Mrs. Bowman that she would not forget to douse them when we left. I do not recall that Mrs. Bowman held any religious beliefs that would give her reason not to use electricity, or if it were merely the fear of it that caused her to shun such a modern convenience, but whatever it was, I for one never relaxed as long as the figures created by the flickering lamplight danced on the dark walls surrounding us, though I tried desperately to keep my mind from thinking about it too long and hard.

Though Mrs. Bowman's daughters were a bit older than my mom, Mom claimed them to have been among her favorite childhood playmates. She recalls that they got along admirably well, though she would have us believe that her role with them was typically that of a bystander. Years later, and only on those occasions when Mom really relaxed into a more talkative mood, would she share some of their youthful escapades which included sliding down Mrs. Bowman's banister. Because the newel post at the base of the stairs featured a finial that greatly restricted their smooth decent into the blankets piled up at the end of their slide, she and the Bowman girls unceremoniously removed the finial, using a sledge hammer retrieved from the woodshed that leaned against the house as if it were too weak to stand on its own.

Then there was the occasion when the girls formed a cake out of dry horse dung, and after frosting it, they placed it by the side of the road in hopes that some unsuspecting motorist would see it and stop to pick it up. Fortunately, no one ever stopped, but unfortunately, Bobby Baker, the neighbor boy who was not in on the ruse and who never met a frosted cake he did not like, took a bite. According to Mom, Bobby shunned cake with chocolate frosting right up to and including the day he died, some sixty years later. And then there were the corn silk cigarettes; empathically, Mom denied ever taking part in smoking the corn silk cigarettes the Bowman girls rolled using the pages of some religious publication and also held fast to her claim that she only witnessed the girls carelessly, but intentionally, use one of those cigarettes to set the orchard on fire just to watch the local firemen scramble to put it out.

I was a teenager when Mrs. Bowman finally passed at the age of ninety-seven. It was an unknown fact, but freely talked about in the neighborhood nonetheless, that the settlement of her estate was hampered by the government's inability to initially locate any of the heirs. Like her husband "Ralphy," they had all disappeared. Eventually located, the siblings put the house up for sale, along with its contents. Rumor had it that pretty much all the money from the sale went to pay back taxes, something Mrs. Bowman felt was a totally ridiculous use of money, so she never paid them.

Local lore had it that the house's new owners, deciding to capitalize on its history, opened it as a haunted house. Initially, this prompted visits from those who relish such supernatural aberrations, and the reports emanating from those encounters grew to include visitors hearing childlike laughter coming from the stairs, occasional strains of piano music coming from the music room, and sightings of ghostly figures dancing around the dining room and the parlor at night. But soon such novelty wore off, and because the few daring souls who would venture in from time to time were not enough to sustain it, the business failed, putting the new owners into foreclosure. It was then purchased by a gentleman who was eager to turn it into a zoo of sorts that would feature unusual jungle animals, but it, too, failed when for some unexplained reason a number of the animals died or disappeared, and the home's owner ran into some financial difficulty of his own. For many years the house stood empty amid a growing fortress of scrub and brush. I still get an eerie feeling each time I pass by that location, even though I try desperately to keep my mind from thinking about it too long or too hard.

ELEVEN

Character #3- Mrs. Van Drunen

If you want to succeed in life... always be you!!! You are who you are when nobody's looking.

-Unknown

THROUGH THE EYES AND MIND of anyone, the Van Drunens would be considered an odd couple, to say the least. As far as I was concerned, though, they were just another in a long line of "characters" my mom made a point to "stop and look in on" from time to time. In my nine-year-old estimation, they epitomized the Jack Sprat nursery rhyme; Mr. Van Drunen had no fat on his skeletal 6'4" frame, and Mrs. Van Drunen had no lean on a frame the height of which was difficult to determine as it seemed to have melted into a large puddle that kept molding and remolding itself in, around, and through the confines of the wooden cushion-less chair that bore her weight from sun up until sun down. Even Mr. Van Drunen, never given to too much conversation due to his heavy Dutch accent and his frequent inability to get a word in edge-wise anyway, would affectionately describe her as "someone who was too heavy for light work and too light for heavy work." I recall whispering to one of my friends, out of earshot of my parents, of course, that Mrs.

Van Drunen was as big around as she was tall and that perhaps she always found it difficult to pry herself from her perch because, like the piece of barbed wire that over the years our big maple tree had grown around, the chair had actually become a part of her.

When it came to clothing, Mrs. Van Drunen always wore bright floral dresses in tent-like fashion. I reasoned they were designed so as to make getting in and out of them a bit easier, though I could not even begin to imagine how she must have had to struggle to pour herself into them, that is, if she ever managed to get herself out of them. Given their familiar ruffled look, a pretty solid case could be made that perhaps she seldom did. Plopped in the chair, she sat with her two heavily wrinkled stove-pipe sized legs bent to reveal two dimpled knees that long ago had parted ways with each other as they protruded out from under all that material. And all of this was stuffed into a pair of unlaced, like-new, gray orthopedic shoes that, while supporting overlapping ankles, dangled a good six inches from the floor. She looked every bit like the Humpty Dumpty sitting on a wall that I once saw pictured in a nursery rhyme book.

Minus the soup and coffee stains so prevalent among the bouquets of flowers on her dresses, it was bantered about that should the circus, which would frequent our little town from time to time, be in need of another "big top tent," for such a worthy cause, Mrs. Van Drunen would certainly be in a position to provide them with one of hers. I overheard one of my uncles, amid a jovial group of friends, once suggest that her dresses could be used to amply cover any one of his outdoor hay stacks, but I knew he was not serious; after all, a floral tarp would do nothing for his reputation unless, of course, it would help him win a bet. Besides I was not the only one to figure her contribution to a circus would more aptly be that of "the fat lady" side show. It would at least allow her to remain fully clothed and sedentary, two things that seemed to be more suitable to her and everyone else.

Physically, Mrs. Van Drunen bore a neck larger than anyone I had ever seen. Even today's professional body builders would find it hard to hold a candle to its girth. In hushed tones, Mom once told me that it was a goiter and that Mrs. Van Drunen had had it ever since she was a young girl, so I assumed it was something she already knew about, rendering my bringing it to her attention unnecessary; nor would it be polite of me to continue staring at it. Mom also explained, as best she could, that contributing to her obesity, Mrs. Van Drunen had sugar diabetes, and reasoned that because they could not afford the prescribed insulin, she was destined to live with fat but probably not for long. Mom, an expert at extracting a moral from just about any situation, explained that such a malady resulted from eating too much candy, and that if I wished to avoid getting the disease and the shots needed to keep it under control, I would need to limit my intake of sweet things, a threat that still rings in my ears to this day whenever I am tempted by a sweet. But obviously, at the time I was more interested in avoiding that goiter.

I would later learn from those who knew her, that in many ways, Mrs. Van Drunen was her own worst enemy. As it was, when she was still somewhat able to make her way out-of-doors and to the corner drug store, using as her excuse that she was "picking up a daily newspaper," she had also found ways to purchase and consume multiple candy bars while there and on her way home. When such escapades later became nearly impossible due to her inability to move, she would pilfer spoonfuls of sugar from the sugar bowl that enhanced their morning coffee as well as their afternoon kletzs. Both of these indiscretions, my dad reasoned, were contributing factors to her "load of hay set down on two milk cows" physique.

When it came to dress, by contrast, Mr. Van Drunen always wore black pants with a roped-belt and black shirts, all of which draped over his gaunt frame like carelessly hung clothes on a Monday morning wash line. Topped off with an ever present corded and visored black Dutch hat, he looked every bit like a one of those skin-and-bone salt-water worn victims from Davy Jones' locker. Thinking back, I do not recall ever seeing the top of his head, but once having overheard my mom say of it that, "The Lord would not have had to spend a lot of time numbering its hairs," I think I got the picture.

Mr. Van Drunen was prone to get up from his chair and head outdoors without provocation, often in mid-conversation, so perhaps he wore his hat in anticipation of these abrupt and unannounced departures. While going around stocking-footed in the house, Mr. Van Drunen, however, when going out-of-doors, would take time to slip into a pair of wooden shoes before clomping off to wherever it was he felt the urge to go. Actually, I do not recall that he ever went anywhere during these escapes other than to take what seemed to be a leisurely stroll around his yard, bordered by carefully selected treasures rescued from local dump sites. Later, I heard my aunt tell one of her friends that she could understand poor Mr. Van Drunen's need for some time to himself, confessing that Mrs. Van Drunen's relentless whining for things to be brought to or taken from her, "would drive even a preacher to drink."

The Van Drunens lived in a house of economic sacrifices, with rooms too small, ceilings too low—evidenced by moisture laden plasterboard that had just grown tired of clinging to equally exhausted rafters—floors too bare, walls too heavily paneled, and adequately operating bathroom facilities all too absent—the latter being compensated for by an outhouse located at the extremity of the property line and pointed to by a well worn path. Watching Mr. Van Drunen always move about the house bent over so as to avoid contact with the ceiling lights that hung too low and offered too little light, one could, upon entering their home, easily imagine having entered a cave. The house was heated by a pot bellied stove situated in the middle of what was aptly referred to as the living room, which, with the exception of a door-free bedroom, was the only room in the house given the fact that the kitchen and dining areas all merged into each other without boundary. With the exception of a dining room set that featured a large scar-surfaced table with wooden claw-like legs and four mismatched chairs, each in some degree of deterioration; a hutch that displayed long forgotten nick-knacks and took up far too much space when compared to its utility; and Mrs. Van Drunen's favorite chair—the rest of the furniture was made invisible, draped with sundry sheets or blankets. Mom defended this practice by saying that it saved a lot of wear and tear, and should one ever get the urge to redecorate, it was far cheaper to buy a new sheet or blanket than to buy new pieces of furniture or reupholster the old ones. I guess that made sense, but I do not recall that the Van Drunen's ever redecorated.

As the stories about this couple grew in both size and dimension, every bit like those known to revolve around one's fishing prowess, there was one such story that stood out more than the others. They say that fact is stranger than fiction, and perhaps nothing would prove this hypothesis more than the day that Mr. Van Drunen suffered what appeared to be a heart attack.

As the story goes, Mr. Van Drunen awoke one morning and, not feeling well, complained to Mrs. Van Drunen that he was feeling tightness in his chest. Assuming that no one suffered as much as she did, and because it was common knowledge that they were as "poor as church mice," which meant that any doctoring and/or hospital visits were to be reserved for matters of emergencies, the determination of which Mrs. Van Drunen reserved for herself, she was quick to diagnose and more than willing to offer medical advice when it came to her husband's health complaints. To address this particular complaint, her prescription was to, "Just put on the coffee and cut me some wood, and if you're still not feeling well, then lie down for a while until it passes."

Having long ago come to the conclusion that "Ma knows best," or having resigned to the futility of arguing differently, Mr. Van Drunen usually did as he was told. Before heading outdoors with axe in hand, he dutifully placed the coffee pot on the stove, slipped on his wooden shoes, and headed for the back yard where earlier that fall a Good Samaritan had dragged a goodly number of oversized logs to be chopped into firewood for use in their potbellied stove.

As more time passed than such a task typically would require, and there was still no sign of her husband, Mrs. Van Drunen managed somehow to maneuver her chair to the kitchen window overlooking the backyard and peering out of it, she witnessed her worst fear. There on the lawn in a contorted but still recognizable prenatal position lay the body of Mr. Van Drunen.

As the story continues, upon seeing this, Mrs. Van Drunen literally sprang to her feet, and with her chair still attached, she ran out the front door unaware that her bad knees were supporting both her bulk and that piece of furniture without complaint. Ignoring what she considered to be her husband's corpse, she hastily waddled in the direction of the nearest neighbor, who lived less than a football field's length away, to seek help and access to a phone. Although they had always intended to install a phone of their own, they had never gotten around to it. How she managed to maneuver such a distance with that piece of furniture still a part of her, no one to this day can explain, but as the story continues to unfold, upon arriving at the neighbors' and breathlessly relating the tale, she managed with equal speed to retrace her steps with both the neighbor fellow and that piece of furniture following close behind.

Arriving back in the yard and hopeful that the distant siren was heading in their direction, the neighbor hurriedly knelt to inspect the body and was surprised to find that Mr. Van Drunen was actually still breathing and seemed to just be asleep. Shaking him awake, Mrs. Van Drunen screamed at her husband, "Are you okay?" Seemingly confused, he sheepishly replied that he was fine. "What are you doing on the ground then?" she queried, still more than a bit hysterical. "I am resting," was his matter-of-fact reply. "What do you mean you're resting?" Her questioning now featured more anger than angst. Nonplussed, he replied, "Well, you told me if I did not feel better after I put on the coffee and chopped the wood that I should rest." What she said next I was not privy to, but I assumed that was because the adults in my life at that time did not want to be a stumbling block to my innocence. Even though death has long ago claimed both of these characters, whenever I recall them, I confess to feeling a bit sorry for Mr. Van Drunen; after all, he was only doing what he was told, but knowing Mrs. Van Drunen, I doubt seriously that he ever got any credit for it.

TWELVE

Character #4 - Charlie Free

If you're in trouble or hurt, or in need- go to the poor people. They're the only ones that'll help- the only ones.
-John Steinbeck

CHARLIE FREE WAS YET ANOTHER of those types my mom would affectionately refer to as a "character" and though at the time of this writing he has been gone a goodly number of years, whenever his name would come up in conversation, it is quite apparent Mom had scrapbooked only the fondest memories of this little Frenchman. Long considered a friend and neighbor, Charlie first appeared on Mom's family farm as a hired man whose initial employment was necessitated by the sudden passing of my mom's father. At the time, my mom was only eight months old, and given the fact that Charlie pretty much showed up for some portion of work almost every day since being hired, for a long time my mom was convinced that Charlie was her "dada." She continued to believe that, that is, until Grandma remarried when my mom was not quite four years old, and suddenly there was someone new in the family who insisted on being called "Father."

While it was well known that Charlie was not the sort one could always depend on, nor was the work that he did manage to do always done in the most effective and efficient manner, which combined to make his tenured employment anywhere always a bit tenuous at best, it was pretty obvious from the very beginning that "Father" had no intention of competing with him for the attention and devotion of his newly acquired brood. Thus, it came as no surprise to the neighborhood when shortly after the wedding ceremony, Charlie's employment was terminated. Though anticipated, the actual reason for his firing continued to provide ammunition for the various town coffee battalions until such time as all had done battle with it and eventually surrendered to the same conclusion that "Father" just wanted to get his hands on Grandma's farm.

My mom recalls missing Charlie terribly after his being let go, a fact that Grandma would validate when reminiscing how Mom would sit on the window sill in the family dining room every morning for months watching and waiting for Charlie to come walking up the driveway and wave at her on his way to the barn as he had done so many times before. Such vigils would typically end with Mom in tears, requiring a goodly measure of Grandma's reassurance that Charlie had not abandoned her.

Coincidently, it was shortly after Charlie's dismissal that local farmers began to notice the mysterious disappearance of a bale of hay now and again from their storage areas and the mysterious appearance of little piles of grain on their storage floors, obviously left by someone in careless haste. Collectively, it was suspected, but never pursued, that it might be the work of Charlie, now unemployed, who probably was prowling around to feed the two humongous work horses that shared his ten- acre homestead. Those horses, Charlie would always announce with a certain amount of bravado to anyone who would listen, were a gift he had given himself to commemorate his one day of wedded bliss to the club-footed Hassel Baxter, who had married him one afternoon only to leave him before breakfast the very next day. "I bought those horses with all the money I figured I'd be savin' not being married," he would chuckle. But those who knew him knew that a part of Charlie left with his bride that day.

Why Charlie felt the need for such beasts of burden remains to this day a mystery among those who remember him. After all, they reasoned, there certainly was no practical use for them on Charlie's land, infertile as it was, except for the uninvited and equally unattended growth of shrubs and brome grasses that took up residence there and admirably functioned to camouflage a minefield of field stones. The only conclusion that made any sense at all to the folks in town was that Charlie's hay burners provided him with a measure of companionship.

As everyone suspected, Grandma's second marriage, like Charlie's first, would eventually prove to be a mistake. Two additional children and four years later, after trying to make a go of it, Grandma gave up, and my mom found herself without her "dada" or a "Father." A moonshiner, who fully believed in sampling his own product, "Father" apparently had gotten "funny" one too many times as far as Grandma was concerned. Though she weighed in at slightly less than ninety-five pounds and stood barely five feet tall with a strand of braided pitch-black hair that ran down her back of nearly equal length, she, nevertheless, was a determined little woman. Despite being ecclesiastically opposed to divorce under any circumstance, Grandma—having finally become convinced that her new husband was not only up to no good, but truly was no good—used the tined ends of a pitch fork to urge "Father" in the direction of the road with a stern admonition that he never set foot on her property again. Despite the fact that no one ever recalled seeing "Father" on or near Grandma's property again, his presence, though never proven, was speculated, given the mysterious deaths of a number of Grandma's pigs and chickens, which the local vet, who doubled as the family doctor, determined to have been the result of some sort of poisoning.

To my mom's delight, one morning shortly after word got around that the little "Jewish" woman at the end of the mile had finally extricated her freeloading husband, Charlie came walking up the drive.

Despite his overall appearance looking more disheveled than Mom had remembered, and despite the fact that his face was now almost completely hidden behind a mass of unpruned facial hair which hid the twinkle she always seemed to be able to coax from him, as far as Mom was concerned, Charlie never looked better. Grandma, on the other hand, was overheard telling a neighbor that the years had not been kind to Charlie, evidenced by the fact that though barely fifty-five years of age, his speech and pace had slowed even more. However, prompted by sheer need and perhaps a touch of sympathy, Grandma rehired Charlie on the spot, and even though it now took him longer to complete even the simplest of tasks, ironically, the thefts in the neighborhood strangely subsided. "That alone should be worth something," Grandma confessed in whispers to those she knew would hold her confidence even though she was never convinced of the connection. However, eventually, even the family pastor would come to credit Grandma with single-handedly saving Charlie from a life of crime and, as a consequence, perhaps his very soul from eternal damnation. Although "pulpit-ly" opposed to divorce, this man of the cloth secretly confessed to Grandma that he was sure that God would wink at her divorce in lieu of this greater good.

Soon it was as if Charlie had never left. Upon arriving in the morning and waving at Mom sitting on the sill, he would disappear, doing whatever he did out from under watchful eyes. Mom recalls that Charlie never owned a watch as he said he had no need of one. Grandma tended to agree with Charlie's conclusion, convinced that he possessed some sort of internal mechanism that would at least alert him to mealtimes, given his uncanny propensity to appear in the house around such times. The scene would then unfold as if scripted. Peering at the only clock in the house which perched atop a slotted ledge intended for the display of fancy plates, Charlie would open by exclaiming, "Oh my gosh! Would you look at that? Where does the time go? I had no idea that it was already lunch time," which would always be followed by Grandma's sincere invitation for him to join the family in a repast to which, as if on cue, Charlie's equally predictable response would always be, "Well, if you do not think I'd be imposing...."

That particular clock required daily winding, a task, which when Grandma remembered to do it, would find her precariously standing on a chair using a needle-nosed pliers she had confiscated from the tackle box "Father" had abandoned in his haste to avoid being run through. Ever since one of Mom's younger brothers had pirated and then lost the key intended for such windings, the pair of pliers was called into duty as a substitute, and while no one could ever be quite sure of the clock's accuracy, it continued to regulate life on the farm. Nevertheless, Grandma used to say that while she would never know when Charlie would show up for work, she could always set the clock to his mealtime appearances.

Typically lacking in hygiene, Charlie did little to improve matters with his new beard which often recorded the residue of past meals and tracked the spillages of various liquids, which made it quite repulsive to others though it seemed of no consequence to my mom, now nearly nine years of age. She recalls sitting on Charlie's lap while Grandma would busy herself with last minute meal preparations and listen to Charlie spin yarns that enthralled my mom enough to announce that when she grew up, she would marry him, a proclamation that never failed to send Charlie into a fit of laughter. But Mom remained steadfast to her covenant until such time as her affections gradually evolved, with the passing years, into mere playful flirtation and then rightfully and unceremoniously faded away completely after meeting my dad at eighteen and marrying him a couple of years later. However, even after my mom pledged her troth and birthed four boys, Charlie managed to remain a part of our family. And though he had long ago lost his desire and ability to work, he never lost that sixth sense when it came to mealtime; consequently, he would often be a guest at our family table as well.

Officially retired, Charlie came to understand the impracticality of keeping his horses which were now "older than dirt." One day he announced that he might as well get something for them before he would have to drag them out of the barn "as stiff as long underwear on a winter clothesline." Overhearing the remark that "those old horses were only good for glue," my mom recalls taking some solace in the belief that those horses might come to a better end than that when, with childlike innocence, she determined it to be quite impossible for something so big and brown to become something so sticky and white, much less fit into a glue bottle.

Years after retiring his horses, which mercifully just disappeared one day, Charlie also announced the retirement of his "Fliver"- a term he used to affectionately refer to his broken-down car of questionable vintage, presumed to have been paid off from the proceeds of the sale of those horses. Though the car was seldom road worthy, Mom said it probably was a good thing that Charlie, now nearing eighty, had decided to give up driving when he did, not so much because he could no longer hear or see very well, but because the town had recently up and gone "big city" by hiring its own constable, and it was pretty common knowledge that Charlie never possessed a driver's license. Perhaps it dawned on him that getting along in age; he was too old to risk spending what was left of his life in jail.

A neighbor, who looked in on Charlie from time to time, found him one day sitting at his kitchen table with his Bible open to the Book of Revelations and his head resting on his arms as if he had merely fallen asleep. Since no one really saw reason to pin-point the time of his death or the cause of it, the local newspaper merely reported that Charlie Free, age eighty-one, give or take a year or two, died of natural causes, though my mom would never be convinced that he did not die of a broken heart he never allowed anyone to see.

Suffice it to say, the tales embroidered into the local lore concerning Charlie Free still find their way into community conversations from time to time. It was not that long ago that I followed up such a conversation with my mom concerning Charlie by taking a nostalgic drive past what everyone, including Charlie, figured to be his old homestead. As the story goes, however, official records eventually revealed that Charlie never really owned his place; rather, he just sort of squatted on it after the disappearance of its previous owner. Apparently, no one questioned his claim on the property back then, assuming he was somehow an heir of the former owner even though the records would eventually show that the former owner was of first generation Polish descent. It seems that since Charlie had dutifully paid the property taxes, often a year or two in advance, the county apparently never had reason to question anything. This situation came to light, however, two years after Charlie's death when the prepaid taxes caught up with the year in question, and a subsequent mandated audit revealed that while Charlie had no known heirs, neither did the former owner.

For years, a contorted and faded "For Sale" sign feebly testified to the county's desire to sell the property that had stood vacant since Charlie's death. Almost completely devoured by subsequent generations of those same shrubs and brome grasses that originally grew up there, the house and outbuilding bore irrefutable witness to the many years of neglect. As for Charlie's "Fliver," over the years it had grown tireless and rusted beyond reclamation. A twisted crabapple tree had somehow managed to take up residence through its hoodless engine while a number of errant thistles and white daisies had opted for living space in its lidless trunk. As it was, until someone actually purchased the property quite some time ago, Charlie's "Fliver" continued to crouch in the landscape as if it were keeping an eye on the place in Charlie's absence in anticipation of the day when he would come walking up the driveway, and life would once again be as it was.

THIRTEEN

Mom

There's a story behind everything, but behind all your stories is always your mother's story...because hers is where yours begins.

-Mitch Albom

ACCORDING TO A 2009 SURVEY, 70% of American families feature a working mom, and by 2010 it was predicted that for the first time in our nation's history, the majority of our work force will be made up of women. But long before it became popular to trade motherhood for the things believed to be needed to assuage our media-salted thirst, my mom defined and epitomized what it meant to be a "stay-at-home working mom." There is little doubt that her future was shaped at a very young age by the Depression, which required her to forgo the expense of schooling, and hence any hope for a career, in exchange for putting food on her family's table. Poverty puts everyone "at risk," and my mom's family was no exception. Growing up during these depressed times on a small farm with three blood and two step-siblings in a fatherless home necessitated survival ingenuity devoid of life's little extras. Having had to leave school for financial reasons upon completing the sixth grade (and one additional year helping the 6th grade teacher in seventh grade), Mom worked picking fruit in season and cleaning houses to help supplement the family coffers. Despite the fact that her life was molded in a crucible of premature adult-like responsibilities, Mom's "good memories" continued to far outdistance her unfulfilled dream of being a school teacher, though there is little doubt, even into her nineties she would have made a good teacher. As it was, she graciously chose the life of a farmer's wife without complaint and taught Sunday school longer than any tenured pastor, all the while taking particular delight in raising us children and always supporting and encouraging us in our own schooling. She was convinced it would guarantee us an "easier life."

In many ways, like her spinster sister three years older than she, Mom grew to be fastidiously religious in her attempts at orderliness and cleanliness, perhaps both having something to do with her deep faith and the connection she made between cleanliness and godliness. As we were growing up, one of her threadbare admonitions was, "It doesn't have to be new, as long as it is clean." My brothers and I always felt she used it as way to make us feel guilty for relentlessly negotiating for new and branded clothing while people in Africa were not only starving but running around naked; and if that were not enough to convince us, her ace in the hole was her rather loose translation of the biblical truth that "man cannot live by bread alone" which, she managed to somehow convince us, also meant our not needing to purchase new clothes, unless, of course, it was absolutely essential. To compensate for worn out apparel, Mom specialized in darning and patching, which would not have been half so bad if the darning (a portion of this word Mom made sure we only utter in reference to the mending of socks) or patching would in any way match the color and texture of that which was in need of it. Eventually, such darning and patching came to be considered fashionable; unfortunately, such was the case long after we kids had grown and had children of our own. It still gives me pause whenever I think that Mom, who earned every penny she saved, might well have been an unrecognized and unappreciated trend-setter.

The idea that the Joneses were not people in need of nor worthy of being kept up with was a corollary belief of Mom's. The admonition that one's wallet, if unbridled, would lead one astray certainly would have been a sermon wasted on my mom. On the other hand, being no stranger to the use of needles, the parable about the camel and the rich man certainly must have resonated with her as she seemed intent that while other things might serve to keep her out of Heaven, possessions would not be one of them. Always having taken a great deal of pride in "marching to the beat" of the Holy Book, she was a master at wasting not despite our wanting. Perhaps I am no exception to the unwritten rule that every kid growing up is embarrassed by his parents at one time or another for one reason or another, because more often than not such thrift made me feel ill at ease, especially among my peers. To that end, I recall my displeasure at having to wear hand-me-down bibbed overalls to elementary school when all the other kids wore new belted jeans or slacks. I could never understand why I had to carry my school lunch in a used syrup can when everyone else carried an officially sanctioned *Lone Ranger* or *Sky King* lunch-box with matching thermos, nonetheless! I could not make sense as to why my sandwiches had to feature baked beans and cow tongue when everybody else's was made of store bought lunch meat or peanut butter and jam. I envied those with *Twinkies* and was embarrassed, and perhaps on occasion a bit peeved, when no one would trade their *Twinkie* for my piece of apple sauce cake, the frosting of which too often would mysteriously melt into the cake, or if there would happen to be any of it left on the cake, most of it would relentlessly cling to the waxed paper once it was removed. I resented the fact that each year on my first-day-of-school I carried re-sharpened remnants of both crayons and pencils in a used cigar box still reeking of its intended contents and bearing the picture of a long-haired guy wearing a feathered hat and whose neck was being supported by some sort of a frilly corrugation. Meanwhile, by stark contrast, the other kids sported fancy boxes of brand-new 64 *Crayolas* accompanied by never-before sharpened #3 pencils housed in plastic holders with sliding covers featuring rulers with sharpeners.

As I grew older, the difference between how my parents did things and how things were done by the rest of the world became even more apparent to me. I do not recall exactly when I made the discovery that not everyone's bed linens were made from bleached feedbags or that laundry soap came granulated in a box rather than peeled from homemade cakes made of lye and lard. My discovery of a real tub with a shower dispensed with the idea that everyone took a bath in the sink or the milk house and, of course, there was the outhouse issue. Looking back, I am convinced that my parents would have been more at home had they been born into an Amish family during the mid-1800s as both seemingly took undue pride in not only their humility but their simplicity as well.

With the exception of her Sunday best, Mom's daily attire would be plain but typically offset with colorful aprons and matching bonnets always hand-made from left over materials. "Quaint" is how she was affectionately referred to by those who knew her, as well as those who did not; "odd" is how I felt. But we were loved, and we laughed a lot, and as long as we were not in public that seemed to be sufficient compensation for what I deemed to be our family's less than contemporary approach to life.

I recall that another of Mom's clean and neat rituals required the walls, ceiling, and attic of our home to undergo serious fall and spring cleanings, necessitated, she reasoned, by the reality of the coal and wood burning furnace in our Michigan cellar. During this time of purification, everything had to be moved and washed down with a mixture of ammonia, *Pine Sol, Borax* and vinegar. When the daunting multi-day task was finally completed to Mom's satisfaction, I could never understand how things seemed to look no different than before we had started given the color of the cleaning water we threw out the backdoor. With the exception of my wrinkly fingers and uncharacteristically clean cuticles, I saw little benefit in the exercise. Years later I made my peace with it, coming to realize that it must have been very important for Mom to know that everything had undergone a baptism that, for a time at least, cleansed things of their dust and dirt. By her sister's admission, Mom was not only a master of clean but also of organized chaos; her domain could be likened to a jigsaw puzzle, in that while everything had a place and everything might eventually wind up in it, to everyone else there were pieces missing and very little seemed to fit together.

The extent of Mom's fastidiousness did not stop at the doors of our home. For over thirty years, as a member of a *TOPS* club (Take Off Pounds Sensibly), she voluntarily took on the responsibility of "adopting the mile," which meant that she picked up the trash along the mile long stretch of the road in front of our home on behalf of the *TOPS* organization; this is something she did until doing so required more of her than her body was willing to give. While such benevolence could be viewed from a perspective of it being yet another opportunity to salve her natural bent, Mom confessed that her motivation for joining the organization, composed of those suffering from "another disease of affluence," was for a far different reason. *TOPS* is a program specifically designed for those who are overweight to lose weight, not only to realize their desire to look better but in many case as a necessity to actually feel better. Like most 12-step programs, it requires accountability and mutual moral support to, from, and among its membership. Needless to say, Mom's 120 pound 5'2" frame allowed her to spend more time giving than receiving such support, and more importantly, it afforded her an opportunity to shine like a beacon of virtue amidst a massive sea of unwanted flesh and pounds, something for which she took a great deal of delight. In the club's "before" and "after" photos, Mom always stood out as an "after" even before there was an opportunity for others in the group to evolve that way by sweat, diet, and unfaltering determination.

Daily, as weather and health permitted, Mom would walk the mile bearing the sign giving recognition to the *TOPS* club for its intention and commitment to keep the mile free of debris. Dressed in her typical garb, that never failed to elicit the question of curious strangers as to whether or not she truly was an "Amish woman," Mom would pick up the discards of careless passers-by. This she would do without fanfare, assuming that it was what any good citizen would do for their country. However, on one particular day while on her circuit, she encountered a dilemma that everyone who knew her knew would challenge yet another of her strongly held ideals.

Dad, though far from being the demonstrative type and typically adhering to a strict economy of words, nevertheless, loved to tell the story how on that particular day as Mom walked her mile, she noticed something shiny in the ditch. At first glance, to her glee, it appeared to be another opportunity for a $.10 refund; however, upon closer examination, she determined that the glint emanated from a six-pack of unopened beer. You have to understand that for my mom, there were only a few things worse than trash along "her" road, and one of those things was anything that had to do with alcohol, having grown up in a fatherless home as a direct result of it. Her own mother had so successfully driven home the point of its evilness, that my mom would feign to touch anything even remotely associated with it, hence the making of a dilemma. There was trash in "her" ditch, but it was of the sort that featured evil spirits armored in aluminum. What to do? Dad relates that Mom, finding a branch nearby, was unsuccessfully trying to use it to dislodge the cans from their resting place by poking the tip of the branch through the plastic rings that bound them when a truck she recognized approached along the road. It was our neighbor, a gentleman well known in our little town to be less squeamish about such things. Mom, flagging him down and explaining the whys and whereabouts of the problem, asked him if he would be so kind as to retrieve the cans and take care of them for her. This he did, and following extensive expressions of Mom's gratitude, both continued on their way.

Having finally completed her route, Mom returned home only to be greeted by a continuation of her previous squeamish encounter. There on the front porch, perched as if on display for all to see, was the six-pack that her neighbor had taken care of, but not in the way Mom had intended or expected him to. Embarrassed that any one of her egg customers or casual visitors might have seen this display and equally fearful that if they had not they might, Mom hurried to the barn to elicit Dad's help in properly disposing of it. Such incriminating evidence could well serve as a potential threat to her reputation of not only having nothing to do with such impropriety but also for speaking so adamantly against it. Dad, himself a teetotaler, either by nature or Mom's nurture, recalls specifically asking her how best to do this, to which she gave her typical reply whenever queried as to what to do with the likes of anything organic, such as table scraps, spoiled milk, or moldy bread: "Feed it to the chickens." Dad admits that he took seriously Mom's "waste not want not mentality" and innocently concluded that perhaps even beer was capable of serving a useful purpose, not to mention the added bonus that the empty containers would afford when redeemed for cash.

A couple of days passed, and during one of those mid-morning discussions at the kitchen table while sipping a second cup of coffee and munching on a piece of my mom's chocolate cake, Dad recalls Mom sharing with him her concern that there might not be enough eggs to satisfy the needs of her customers by week's end. She explained that for some reason, unbeknown to her, the chickens had uncharacteristically lowered their production. In an effort to determine why this might be so, Dad suggested that perhaps it might not have been a good idea to feed the beer to the chickens. Further exploration of that possibility revealed that Dad had not only poured the contents of the cans into the chicken's water dispenser, he did so undiluted. Despite Mom's critical evaluation of how Dad had handled the matter, there was no way they were able to avoid the hilarity of the situation. Both rolling in laughter, they began relating incidences of their having recently seen the chickens wandering aimlessly and on occasion falling over though they gave little thought at the time to how strange this was or what might have caused it. As the story goes, despite the temporary loss of some revenue due to the apparent result of something that had gone afoul in the hen house, about a week later the hens' production of eggs returned; however, those eggs that before were typically candled as small and medium were now weighing in as large and jumbo. Whenever Dad would relate this story, which he often did when Mom deserved some teasing or he needed to "get even," he would end it with the threat of repeating the stunt and changing the "Eggs for Sale" sign out front to read "Eggnog in a Shell for Sale," and to the amazement of the listeners, Mom would go along with the idea, agreeing that it just might sell. But then again, as they say, "When you know what you know for sure, you can afford to play along"…and everyone, including Dad, knew who ruled the roost in our house.

FOURTEEN

Sports

All work and no play makes Jack a dull boy.
-Proverb

WHILE IT WOULD BE NEARLY impossible to pinpoint exactly how or when my interest in sports (and baseball, in particular) began, if I had to guess, I would have to say it was my older brother who sparked and fanned the initial flames of my passion for the games. With a five year head start on me, and still somewhat innocent when it came to the economical benefits he could reap from hard work, on occasion my older brother could be seen playing with Dad's old baseball glove and a stitch-frayed baseball he had found near the high school athletic field where it had obviously been lost and forgotten in the tall grass of foul territory.

While tossing the ball up on the roof of our house, he would vocalize, as if sports casting, how it had been drilled there off the bat of the likes of Mickey Mantle, Frank Robinson, Ted Williams, or Duke Snider. Unless such tossings resulted in the ball going over the other side of the roof, which usually meant I would have to go and fetch it having been dubbed the designated retriever, my brother would field it coming off the roof, and in dramatic fashion, wheel and make an imaginary throw to an imaginary base after which he would pump his fist in the air to celebrate an equally imaginary game-ending twin-killing. When the day finally came that his tossings required more and more retrievals, I finally donned a glove of my own, one I had recently found discarded in the local dump. It featured a webbed backstop, a well worn deep pocket, and five fingers, which though intended to be woven together, splayed independent of each other due to the absence of a strip of rawhide. I was able to remedy this minor inconvenience by using a shoestring from one of my dad's discarded barn boots that, despite being filled with labor intensive holes, had been designated as potential patching material and thus spared the burning barrel. Standing on the other side of the house in anticipation of an appearance by the ball, I thought our game took on all the attributes of Eenie-Einine-Over, limited only by my ability to always throw it hard and high enough to actually crest the peak of the roof. This was something that irritated my brother to no end, but no less so than on those occasions when the ball would get hung up in the eaves trough, forcing us to obtain a ladder from the tool shed in order to retrieve it. Such interruptions not only substantially slowed the progress of our play but also reduced the amount of time we had for it.

As summer would fade into fall, my brother might be seen fidgeting with a rather lopsided football made so by a portion of its bladder peeking through an unsutured fracture in its outer skin. Tossing the football high into the air, he would pretend it had been spiraled there from the hands of quarterbacks the likes of Y.A. Title, Kyle Rote, Frank Gifford, or Johnny Unitas. His imagination would then allow him to intercept such loftings from the clutches of would-be receivers, and then dashing between evil intentioned tacklers, he would head toward some imaginary end zone for the game-winning touchdown. Upon crossing the equally imaginary goal line, he would dramatically spike the ball in a fashion still copied by pro football players to this very day.

Having on another occasion visited the city dump, I rescued a hard cardboard-like football helmet minus a face guard, which it was never intended to have, but it too lacked a number of stitches which it was intended to have. By replacing its missing stitches, I was able to restore it to near store-bought quality, which punched my ticket to play with the "big boys" in the neighborhood. Even though my assignment typically was only that of the designated blocker, I did not mind; after all, I was the only one who "looked like a real football player," what with the re-stitched helmet, a white t-shirt on which I had scrawled the number "7" with black crayon, and my "shoulder pads," which I formed with two of Dad's rolled up flannel shirts, that frustratingly required repositioning after almost every play. Eventually, some of my other talents were recognized, and I was promoted to all-time hiker, but by the time I had honed my skills enough to be considered for one of the really important positions, the "big boys" were playing the real thing in middle school and no longer had the time nor interest in playing with "little kids."

As fall would give way to winter, my brother would busy himself moving the harvested hay bales that hibernated in the loft of our barn. He would create a space wide enough to provide a clear path to the backboard-less basketball hoop we had nailed to one of the barn's interior girders. If this were not challenging enough, the game was made all the more difficult by the net-less hoop positioned at a guesstimated height and tilting slightly to the right while sagging slightly toward the floor. While all this made for an interesting target, the fact that our basketball featured a slow leak, which required it to be pumped up prior to the start of any play and on more than one occasion during it, made the game all the more challenging. This slow but sure deflation, combined with sub-freezing temperatures and the narrow pathway leading to the basket, not only severely restricted our ability to dribble-in for a layup around the imaginary out-stretched hands of the likes of Jerry Lucas, Bob Cousy, Elgin Baylor, or Bob Pettit, but it also forced our shot selection to the perimeter and our scoring to whoever would win the arguments as to whether the ball actually had penetrated the hoop or just passed near it.

Somewhere along the line even little kids grow up, and their fantasies give way to the realities of organized sports, making their games so much more competitive and less fun to play. In the particular time and place I found myself as a teenager, the only three middle and high school sports "the true jocks" would be caught dead playing were football, basketball, and baseball. Since I had played all of them in the friendly confines of our neighborhood environment, as well as had exposure to their rules and nuances, one would think my transition into them would have been easier than it actually was. Upon starting middle school, I anticipated going out for football, as did most of my buddies, with the exception of those who opted to join the band or hang out with the "hoods" and smokers in the parking lot. Talk among my sports-minded peers centered mainly around who would play what position, for we had little concern about not making the team since the sheer numbers required in football put the emphasis on recruiting rather than on cutting.

My first exposure to organized football practice came on a day when the temperature hovered over 100 degrees, a fact that, to this day, I credit with my shortened career. Having heretofore played pick-up flag football in the neighborhood—and always within a short distance of someone's refrigerator that typically featured iced lemonade or some other beverage—nothing had prepared me for the heat and actual physical contact of contact sports. Though I recall thinking that as a farm boy I should have been hardened to these sorts of things, even before the first practice evolved into the second, I hung up my helmet and left the jocks on the field in favor of the fans in the stand. Using my heart murmur as an alibi, I was able to avoid the stigma assigned to those who chose not to play the game in lieu of their instruments of sound or smoke.

Basketball came next. Again, I tried out for the team, this time knowing full well that cuts would be a reality. Fortunately, I made the bench team, a position I played quite well all through middle and high school. As it was, my 5'10" frame slotted me for a guard position, which just happened to be replete with upper and lower classmen. Unfortunately for me, these players' homes were equipped with pro-sanctioned, fully inflated basketballs and featured netted baskets appropriately measured and mounted onto garages situated on cement driveways. Perhaps because I had an average perimeter shot, which many years later was elevated to the status of a three-pointer, and because I played an adequate defense, I would occasionally sub for one of the starting guards, but only when the coach's concern for their mounting fouls exceeded the risk he felt he was taking by putting me on the floor. Since almost every play in our team's arsenal meant getting the ball to our 6'2" and 6'3" inside men, the value of the outside guys was limited, making my contribution even more situational and insignificant. In 1964, my senior year, our team was affectionately referred to in the Grand Rapids newspapers as their local "Cinderella" team. As it turned out our little collection of farm boys surprised everyone by making it to the big dance – the Class C Basketball State Finals. We suffered a loss in the final foray, and while even to this day the community continues to take a great deal of vicarious pride in our accomplishments, I think I was too young to fully grasp its significance and long ago sacrificed my team trophies on the altar of needed space.

At our school's awards banquet that year, I recall being graced with the "Oil Can" Award, a designation which bore visual evidence to the fact that my benefit to the team was not in my ability to score or rebound as much as it was in my ability to "fire up" those more adept at doing so. As I am writing this, I recall at the time sharing with my dad, as he was painstakingly laboring to grease and oil the corn binder, my lament for having had to play this role instead of a more major one. He listened patiently to my ramblings and then, without turning away from his undertaking, he philosophized, "A well oiled machine is a well performing machine. Things don't work right or last long if no one takes the time to grease the cogs." And even though now from this vantage point it all seems sort of surreal and insignificant, I am reminded that perhaps my role back then was more important than I gave it credit – even though we all know in our deepest knower that the spotlight favors the rebounders and scorers. Suffice it to say, college found me in the stands cheering on those players more capable of producing both.

Fortunately, I was made for baseball, perhaps a credit to both working on the farm and to my dad, who was, in his own right, born for the game. I was a right-hand thrower by nature and a left-hand hitter by nurture, blessed with a strong arm, a wicked bat, and a sticky glove. I tore up the middle and high school scene with displays of power and hitting for averages that I was sure would have turned the head of any professional scout. Fielding third base or shortstop, I welcomed every ball hit in my direction. The ring finger on my right hand still bears the evidence of one of the few errors I made at those positions. Apparently, my throwing hand got ahead of my glove on a line drive, separating my finger from its nail and requiring it to be taped to prohibit the flesh from dangling beneath it. Though the finger went completely numb in a matter of minutes and somehow managed to encourage the pinkie and middle finger to follow suit, I continued playing the game, hitting a double in the bottom half of the final inning that proved to be the game winning blow. Charlie Hustle had nothing over on me. This time I was "the machine," leaving the role of the "Oil Can" to someone else. In my junior and senior year our team won back-to-back league titles, and my combined four-year contribution featured a .300+ batting average with a half dozen or so HR's and well over fifty RBI's.

I tried out for the baseball team my freshman year of college, and though I made the spring training trip to Florida with the team, going from a full head of hair to a skin head and from top dog to a lowly freshman, who was required to cater to the upperclassmen, was not my idea of fun. Upon my return I opted to give up baseball for my second love, softball. Though claiming my need for self-actualization, I secretly feared the hazing that was so much a part of the Greek scene back then.

So as an Independent, I soon became the feared pitcher of every frat in the college intramural program. Racking up no-hitters and hitting balls for distance were common place occurrences for me, so much so that in my senior year on campus, the Independents won all eight scheduled games, four of which were the result of forfeit. Apparently, our opponents saw little value in showing up for the game.

Graduating from college, I continued to pitch softball in city leagues for thirty plus summers, helping various team sponsors to claim many multi-sized trophies which I imagine have, like all of mine, now been relegated to areas of less conspicuousness. Afraid that I just might be a legend in my own mind, I recently did an archive search at our local library for articles that might bear witness to my remembrances, and while I discovered that the newspapers were not as vigilant in their reporting as I had remembered, I did locate enough articles to at least avoid suspicion. Thankfully, despite the media's lapse, my memories remain intact … so unless someone has been keeping closer track of these things than I have and can show me the box scores, this is and will continue to be my story, and I am sticking to it.

FIFTEEN

Father's Day

*When I was a boy of fourteen, my father was so ignorant
I could hardly stand to have the old man around. But
when I got to be twenty-one, I was astonished at how
much the old man had learned in seven years.*

-Mark Twain

ONCE A YEAR, AT LEAST according to the *Hallmark* calendar, fatherhood
is recognized and in many cases even celebrated. Like most recognized
special days and holidays in our family, Father's Day was often just
"another day at the office." Oh, a homemade card might be shared with
Dad and sentiments for sure, but other than that, there was very little
hoopla and no time off.

Growing up on a farm, it was our reality that each day looked every
bit like the one preceding it, and at no time was this ever more evident
than on those days considered by Hallmark to be special. As far as
our dairy cows were concerned, I am of the opinion they considered
everyday to be a special day, and that meant things ran uninterrupted
according to their schedule. That being the case, while our family
made a point of celebrating most holidays in some fashion or another,

Father's Day, more often than not, would be sacrificed on the altar of daily chores and oversight.

Relating the details of this particular story some years later, Mom admits it all began when she overheard the women in her church's Ladies Aid Guild discussing the fact that Father's Day was coming up. Overhearing their plans for how they were going to make it a special day for their spouses, Mom began to entertain some possibilities of her own. Whether her resolve to celebrate this particular Father's Day was born of guilt for not having done much, if anything, to celebrate this holiday in the past, or if she now considered my two brothers and me to be "old enough" to take part in any plot that might germinate from her contemplations, it was decided that this Father's Day would be different. Little did she know then what we all know now: That this particular celebration would be indelibly written on the pages of our family's lore, there to be revived and retold each year around our own Father's Day table.

As the story goes, Mom composed and directed the details of this particular celebration of Dad's special day with all the skill of a maestro directing an orchestra using an invisible baton. I recall plans being shared in hushed whispers and coded in gestures and facial tics. The secreted plan would see us three boys awakened on Father's Day before Dad would typically be up and about, and without a sound, so as not to disturb him, we were to go to the barn to feed and milk the cows, clean the stables, and see to it that all the other chores were satisfactorily completed while he slept in. It fell to Mom to awaken us and to be sure that when Dad woke up, he would be unable to make his way to the barn. It was a masterful plan—one that demanded precise timing—and because we kids were all in various stages of adolescence, it also proved to require a great deal of physical fortitude and perseverance on our part.

When the day finally arrived, it came as any other, except instead of our alarm clocks going off at 6:30 a.m.—the time we boys would typically get up to help Dad with the chores before breakfast and getting ready for school or church—on this particular day, Mom would quietly awaken us at 5:00 a.m.! Most young boys would prefer that there be only one five o'clock in their day, and it was not the one that came in the morning, and since we were fairly normal adolescents, I recall the three of us grumbling and expressing second and third thoughts about our decision to go along with Mom's scheme as we made our way to the barn in what seemed to be the middle of the night. Meanwhile, Mom had "locked" the bedroom door from the outside so as to give the impression that Dad was barricaded behind it. As accustomed as he was to taking care of his cows, Mom determined that such a strategy would be the only thing that would keep him from doing so on this morning as well.

Though it took a bit longer to accomplish everything without the "Master-of-Milking" having a hand in it, eventually, the three of us completed all of the morning chores, and though we were now feeling more tired than ever, we were also feeling as good about having pulled off the surprise as we were about the possibility of not having to attend the morning church services because of our inability to complete all the work in the typical time it took my dad to complete it on a Sunday.

As the three of us finally left the barn in search of the house, we could see Dad and Mom sitting at the kitchen table sipping coffee and looking quite relaxed. We burst into the kitchen yelling, "Happy Father's Day" with all the enthusiasm we could muster, reminiscent of the surprise Happy Birthday party our family threw for our ninety year old grandmother, nearly sending her into cardiac arrest. We hugged Dad, convinced that we had just done him the biggest favor of his life. Mom, brimming with pride, surveyed the scene and smiled knowingly. It was only years later that she confessed she had to share with Dad what was happening so as to deter him from actually breaking down the door that held him captive.

To say that we were disappointed when Mom and Dad urged us to hurry up because we could still make it to church on time would have been an understatement. We had hoped that after our generous gift of a day off for Dad, we, too, could have a day off from church. But no such luck. I recalled our reluctance in prepping for departure, but it was all for naught; washed and dressed up in our Sunday best, we headed for church on time just as we did every Sunday.

Like our cows who always knew which stanchion was theirs, upon our arrival, we would claim our pre-determined pew and settle in. I recall that each of us boys found ourselves yawning through the announcements, the singing of some opening hymns, and the Scripture readings. If, perhaps, our eyes would close during the sermon, Mom would nudge us awake and give us a dirty look. I found myself wondering about the fairness of it all, for whenever Dad's lids would close, Mom would alibi his doing so by saying he was merely "resting his eyes."

To add insult to injury, it seemed the minister had chosen this particular day to drone on and on about our need to honor our parents so that as obedient children our days might be long in number, and I recall thinking that this day was already long enough. But then, without even pounding the pulpit, he shocked us all when with more than just a tinge of admonition in his voice, he declared "...and next Sunday, being that it will be Father's Day, we have a wonderful opportunity to honor our fathers..." As I caught the look of disbelief in my brothers' eyes and the shock in my mother's, who appeared to be about the business of reassessing her miscalculation, I wondered how Dad might be processing this new information. Not wanting to make eye contact with him, I hazarded a side-ways glance in his direction. He was sitting there with his arms folded, looking straight ahead, and wearing a Mona Lisa-like smile. I wondered if he might be considering the chances of next Sunday looking every bit like this one. Well, it did not.

SIXTEEN

Threshing Days

Life on a farm is a school of patience; you can't hurry a crop or make an ox in two days.

-Henri Alain

IT DAWNED ONE OF THOSE muggy Michigan days when the air felt and smelled like a wet dog or a load of laundry too long ago forgotten in the washing machine. Awakened earlier than usual by my father, who was anxious not to waste a minute of this particular day, I recalled, when the cobwebs had cleared in my head, that I would be spending this day with the threshing crew. I was convinced that this probably ranked right up there on the list of "the last things" a seventeen year old kid with a cool '57 *Chevy*, a steady girl, and a sun drenched sandy beach beckoning from a distance less than twenty miles away, would choose to do, without a parent's mandate.

A threshing bee, though now romanticized in literature and especially by those who have never participated in one, was really hard work. A random collection of uncles and neighbors, whose long days of sun-drenched labor had not only prematurely wrinkled their skin and furrowed their brows but seemingly sobered their approach to life as well, would come together to compose a threshing crew, if the priorities on their own farms permitted. At some point in time, the majority of these men had pooled their hard earned money to purchase and share a slightly used *Harvester-Thresher*. Like a Rube Goldberg creation, it was a monster of a machine that no doubt could have aptly played a lead role in any science-fiction thriller. The machine was engineered to separate the wheat, oats, or spelts from the straw. While the grain would be augured into a grain bin, the bed of a pick-up truck, or a wagon designed for that specific purpose, the straw would be blown into a loft in the barn.

A pulley and belt system, powered by a *Samson* tractor belching black smoke from its single nostril and looking ever so much like an angry bull about to charge, was used to bring this monster machine to life. The results would be a virtual tug-o-war between machine and the tractor that would endure until quitting time. When I was much younger, my uncles were able to convince me that by sitting on this tractor while it droned on hour after hour, I was performing a very important job. A bit older and wiser now, I came to the realization that doing so was meant to keep me out from under the feet of those doing the real work. And even though I would occasionally fall asleep with my head on the steering wheel going nowhere, I was safely out of the way. I recall thinking that it would be nice to have such an easy job to look forward to on this particular day because my assignments had not been that easy for a long, long time.

Annually, the crews and this machine would make the rounds to each other's farm, working as quickly and efficiently as they could so as to take full advantage of favorable weather. They would stop only long enough to grease and oil the machine, make needed repairs, and partake of the enormously popular noon potlucks, compliments of the workers' spouses or significant others. It was common that these ladies would meet together to quilt, sew, or crochet for needy local families or church missions until such time as they would decide it was nearing the dinner hour. Preparations would then commence, and when they were satisfied that everything was ready, they would ring the outdoor dinner bell signaling to the workers to "come and get it."

Despite occasionally tweaking the threshing process over the years, it would not be an exaggeration to state that threshing never was nor ever could be easy or efficient, but it was not for lack of trying. One such ingenious attempt at "modernizing" our procedure would have the straw—typically blown into the barn and haphazardly mowed—blown directly into a baler, thereby producing a more manageable storage option. This procedure allowed threshing to be done in the fields making set-up and take-down so much easier.

As it was, I would start this particular day perched on an empty flatbed wagon. My assigned task was to take the bales birthed by this updated process and strategically stack them on the wagon, which, when loaded, would eventually make its way to storage. Wearing some sort of facial protection to help filter the dust that thickened the air behind the baler never crossed anyone's mind, and even if it had, I doubt seriously my adolescent pride would have allowed me to wear such a contraption. While a pair of sunglasses looked cool, cut the sun's glare, and afforded me with some protection from a portion of the dust and dirt, it also fashioned raccoon-like eyes, exaggerated by the grime that eluded them to the guffawing delight of my fellow crew members. Many of these same guys, when I was much younger, nearly died of laughter as they watched me relieve myself on an electric fence. While frivolity among these typically seriously intentioned workers seldom allowed for comic relief, I could not see why they always seemed to take so much delight in my discomfort.

As wagon followed wagon laden with wheat shocks that eventually would be pitch-forked into the yawning maw of this gorging insatiable threshing monster, I wondered if this particular day would ever end. The fact that I had a date that evening, made things seem to progress even more slowly. Periodically, when the air would clear enough that I could see, I would glance at my watch and angst about whether or not we would finish in time for me to meet up with my date and head off to the beach for an evening dip, which I kept trying to convince myself would at least go a long way to compensate for my spending a hot and dusty day on a wagon behind the baler.

Eventually, the crew finally reached a consensus that it was quitting time, not because the sun had set, but because there were cows in need of milking and other chores that demanded the attention of most of them back at their own farms. I was never so thankful for cows and glad that milking them was not a chore my dad typically now required of me. This task usually fell to my older brother, who to this day remains galvanized in his opinion that he was the most "overworked" of us three kids.

Hearing *Samson* finally wind down to a less obnoxious roar and then gasp for its final breath before things morphed into a much welcomed silence, my plans for the evening seemed salvaged. With the last of the bales having been properly positioned so as to ensure stability in transport, my Uncle Corneal, despite his seventy-eight seasons, slowly but surely made his way to the top of the load. Leaning against the tic-tac-toe framed rack in the front of the wagon and clenching his habitually unlit pipe in the few teeth he still could claim as his own, he positioned himself as if he were holding the reins of an imaginary team of horses. Then with a sound he had perfected and reserved for such times when he actually drove a team of horses, he urged me to "head for the shed" where the wagon would be stored and relieved of its load the following day.

Starting up the small *Farmall* tractor, already hitched to the four-wheeled wagon now laden with bales and Uncle Corneal, I drove out of the field and onto the gravel road leading to the barn and my freedom. The road to our destination featured a rather steep snake-like incline that the kids in the area had grown to appreciate, especially in the winter months when, snow covered and icy, it not only provided some great sledding but also a reasonable excuse for tardiness and absence from the local school. As I began our descent, and feeling the resistance provided by the tractor to the urging of the loaded wagon behind, I recall thinking to myself that if I disengaged the clutch, perhaps things would move along even more quickly. Little did I know how quickly! Without really thinking of the possible consequences, I disengaged the clutch, and the tractor, sensing its freedom and the anxious pushing of the load behind it, quickly gained momentum. And then, as if the wagon were still feeling a bit too constrained, it began weaving and looking every bit like it might be attempting to pass. When the dust finally settled at the bottom of the hill, the tractor and wagon, now facing east-west on a north-south road, had finished the race to the bottom of that hill in a dead heat. In the mayhem, the wagon had been swept clean of its load with the exception of Uncle Corneal, who was clinging to the crossed pieces of the rack looking every bit like someone auditioning for the lead role in a re-enactment of the Crucifixion.

Meanwhile, all the previously animated bales that had somersaulted down the steep slope bordering the road's incline were now resting against briar bushes and swamp shrubs as if trying to catch their breath, some still whole, most fractured. The task of retrieving them was mine and mine alone, which resulted in my hot date giving way to one very long hot evening as bale by bale, fragment by fragment, I reloaded the wagon under the direction of my Uncle Corneal, who I am convinced, felt there was a lesson to be learned in all this. From the perspective of passing time, the good news in all this was that Uncle Corneal lived to the ripe old age of ninety-one, relieving me of any guilt that I might have been the cause of his early demise, and I eventually married the girl whom I stood up on that particular day.

SEVENTEEN

Whitewalls

Vanity and pride are different things, though the words are often used synonymously. A person may be proud without being vain. Pride relates more to our opinion of ourselves; vanity, to what we would have others think of us.

-Jane Austen

SINCE BOTH MY PARENTS KNELT at the altar of, and religiously paid homage to the idea of, not buying anything for which they could not pay cash, I do not recall them ever owning more than one or two new cars in their lifetime, but there was one new car I recall with a great deal of clarity as it was the one that helped launch my legally-licensed driving career. Back then, like most kids nearing their sixteenth birthday, I took Drivers' Education at the local high school thinking it would be a piece of cake; after all, I had been driving around the farm since I was "knee high to a grasshopper," which really meant I was tall enough to reach the pedals and still be able to see through the steering wheel. Drivers' Education was required in order for one to obtain a legitimate driver's license, and so five months shy of my 16th birthday, I enrolled in summer classes. Despite nursing a "been there, done that" superior attitude, it seemed to go pretty well, that is until the day I took my road test with our town cop sitting beside me in the passenger seat. I recall driving out of the school parking lot confident that I had mastered all that needed to be mastered and then some, when a few moments later, he turned to me and asked if I was nervous. There is only one way an adolescent boy can respond to that type of a question in the presence of another male, especially one much older and oozing authority from every pore. "Nope," I confidently replied, hoping to camouflage any uncertainty that might have crept in as a result of my being asked such a question at such a time as this. "Perhaps," he nonchalantly responded, "you're thinking we're in Europe then, but we're not, so you may want to drive on the other side of the road for a while, at least until we get to where we're going." Easing the car back into the more socially and legally accepted lane, I said something that I cannot recall with certainty, but hoped it conveyed that it was never my intent to remain in that lane for any length of time anyway. Then, wanting to be sure that I had covered all my bases, sheepishly I recall admitting that maybe I was a little more unsettled than I thought. As it turned out, I somehow still managed to pass the road test, avoiding what could have been a most embarrassing situation. However, for the next few months, I lived in constant fear that somehow my dad, who was on a first name basis with the town cop—being that his father's father was a second or third cousin to my dad's dad—would become privy to my little indiscretion and that this awareness might restrict any opportunities I might have to drive his new car even though I had officially been sanctioned to traverse the roadways in spite of it.

Dad and Mom's new car was a boxy, shiny black 1962 four-door Rambler, not exactly the type of car that would catch an adolescent's eyes, especially those belonging to someone whose opinion mattered. Nor was it one that would be revered or coveted by those considered otherwise, but it had four wheels, an engine, and smelled new, and for the time being that had to suffice. Once off the showroom floor, the car seldom if ever looked new again, given the fact that the majority of the roads it would have to travel would be of the dirt and gravel variety. Furthermore, our garage, attached to one of the outbuildings, boasted an airiness that seemed to welcome any and all of the elements, not to mention that its dirt floor had over time accumulated a feathery coating of dust such that, no matter how carefully one might drive a newly washed and polished car onto it, the car somehow always managed to emerge enshrouded in a coat of granular brown.

Upon turning sixteen, my maiden solo voyage was to be an evening drive to a school function - a whopping three miles round trip. Only the passage of time has made me truly aware, though, of how much courage this must have taken on my parents' part. Such permission not only posed an economic and health risk, but I was also en route to an encounter with like-minded adolescents for whom speed and showmanship were prerequisites, especially for those interested in climbing the social ladder among their peers, and I admit being one of those. To add to the evening scenario, it was raining, and it must have done so with some intensity during the event because upon leaving, I noticed that the car had shed its earthy coat, and the lights of the parking lot were causing it to glimmer every bit as much as a highly polished gem in a jewelry store window. In hopes that those in charge of social mobility and status at the school would take note of this transformation, as unobtrusively as possible, I drove around the parking lot three times before heading home.

But as one might expect of a teenager driving an adult's car, I was not to be content with the status quo for very long. Soon light-blue angora visor covers were installed, and a pair of equally fluffy and hued dice hung from the interior rearview mirror. While my own personal purchase of a new set of carpeted front floor mats helped to convince Dad to also allow an installation of a new "knicker-knob" featuring a picture of Elvis playing his guitar dressed in his sequins and whites—being the only one my dad would approve of among those I had considered—I was not able to convince him to change out the blackwall tires for new whitewalls. "After all," he reasoned, "these tires have less than 2,000 miles on them, and there's no sense having whitewalls on a farm; it'll be just something else to tend to." It soon became apparent that my begging and pleading would remain entangled in his resolute Depression-like thinking, leaving me to rationalize that maybe all this updating stuff was as futile as rearranging the chairs on the deck of the Titanic or changing the wall hangings in a burning house, for when all was said and done, no matter what I might do, the car would still be a boxy, not-always-shiny black 1962 four-door *Rambler.* But I could not shake the mental volley served up by the counter idea that whitewalls might really help to make the car look somewhat cooler. Eventually, undaunted by Dad's insistence that such a purchase was nothing more than a frivolous use of good money, I began putting my imaginative and resourceful nature to work. I was convinced that if Dad would not buy whitewalls, I could find a way to somehow turn those tires into whitewalls myself.

Scrounging through some of Dad's old paint cans, I found one that read "Oil Based Exterior White." Prying open the rusty lid that time had welded to the can, I found a glob of paint beneath a half-inch crust. I was able to remove the crust only after doing diligence with a screwdriver and hammer. Attempts to stir the glob that remained met with frustration as its consistency could not be altered. This rendered it nearly impossible to dip a paint brush into it much less avoid having paint adhere to the brush in globs once I was finally successful in doing so. I had watched Dad paint the buildings on our farm enough to know that adding paint thinner helps to make paint more pliable. Looking around and failing to find anything of that nature, I recalled that on one occasion Dad used gasoline to perform this thinning miracle. To sate his seemingly always thirsty tractor, Dad had long ago installed an above-ground gas tank, suspended on a bier-like construction, making gas readily accessible, so I decided to give it a go. To my delight, the blending worked, and when my stirrings finally yielded the consistency that could more readily be applied, with all the perseverance and tenacity of an accomplished artist, I commenced painting those portions of the tires that would guarantee a prefect replication of a white wall.

About an hour and a half later and the appearance of the four tires now meeting my expectations for being white walls, I hurried to do my evening chores so I would have time to surprise my then significant other with my handiwork. Once my chores were completed and having obtained the necessary parental permission, I drove to her home with my arm hanging out the window, hair blowing in the breeze, and wearing a facial expression that bespoke an elevated sense of pride in having so ingeniously and economically almost totally transformed the car's personality. But upon arriving at her home, I was in for a rude awakening. You can imagine my horror upon getting out of my car and taking a vanity inspired look-back at my art work, only to discover that the paint must not have been as dry as I had originally thought. Where the tires once featured Rembrandt-like perfect orbs of white, each tire now featured a Picasso-like spatter emanating from the hub caps looking every bit like the rays of a noonday sun. It became pretty evident there was something worse than black-walled tires. Needless to say, without making contact with anyone, I rushed home as quickly as I could with windows closed and looking straight ahead so as to avoid making eye contact with anyone who might happen to be looking my way.

Almost three hours later, after using a gallon of gas, loads of rags, and a whole container of Dad's *Gillette* single-edge razor blades, the tires were scrapped as clean of their whiteness as was humanly possible. Though far from perfect, they were now looking at least somewhat akin to their original nature. It was to be my last alteration of Dad and Mom's new car. Unless, of course, you count the time I did a 180 into the ditch on the curve of one of those ice and snow covered dirt roads and had to be pulled out by some farmer with a tractor, who in his haste, had hooked the tow rope up to the backside of the bumper's undercarriage. As a result, when the rope tightened, it managed to change the appearance of that portion of the car. Fortunately for me,

Dad did not discover this alteration until a couple of months later while washing the car, and upon doing so, he reasoned that he must have driven up too close to one of the posts in the church parking lot. Since he would typically credit all of life's shortcomings and miscues to be the result of original sin as well as count it a privilege to be able to worship such an understanding God who would forgive him for such, he never asked any questions, at least not of me. And because I feared some pretty grave restrictions, I was not about to seek redemption on the altar of confession. It leaves me to wonder what my own children still might not have told me.

EIGHTEEN

Work

I learned the value of hard work by working hard.

-Margaret Mead

AT SIXTEEN YEARS OF AGE, and having determined I needed more money than my dad could wring out of the farm's budget and my uncles from theirs, I began seeking sources of supplementary income. After all, though still a high-schooler, I was now a proud owner of a cool '57 *Chevy* with a steady girlfriend, both in need of constant attention and accessories. Although I was not sure what to expect when I left the security blanket of knowing just about everything there was to know about farming, my naiveté soon came face-to-face with the reality that much of what you learn on a farm, beyond perseverance, does not always translate verbatim to the skills required by other occupations.

When I was much younger, working on our farm was an expectation, appreciated albeit uncompensated. But every once in a while I would be allowed to accompany my dad in making deliveries for the local feed store, one of his supplemental income sources, for which he would usually pay me a quarter or fifty cents. I thought I was pretty big stuff back then riding there with him in the cab of the "big truck," but I never felt as important as on those rare occasions when we would stop at the Pie House—a local watering hole—on our way to or returning from a delivery. My idea of the "real" world was now and then sneaking a sip of Dad's coffee and forking a piece of his mile-high meringue banana cream pie while sitting around well-worn tables with their underlayment of various abandoned wads of Juicy Fruit, Spearmint and an assortment of other gums, while chewing the fat with the locals taking a break. But all too soon those types of jobs were relegated to the place where all my memories of the "good-ole days" go to be embellished. Most of my earlier real-paying jobs were part-time or piece-work. While they were of the type that did not require loyalty beyond the clock or the completion of an assigned expectation, they also did not reward a lot of down time for such things as coffee, pie, and chit chat.

I recall that my first "real" job was doing piecework on a local muck farm where on my days off from school, I, along with a friend, learned how to bag potatoes earning $.05 per 10 lb. bag. The job required little ingenuity or manual exertion, but the tedium was off-set by the fact that I could add up my earnings as I wire-tied each completed bag. However, it was explained to us that because this was seasonal work, it would be a temporary job at best. And so it was that just about the time I had grown efficient enough to earn nearly $2.50 an hour, we ran out of taters.

My next job was also of the seasonal variety and one that almost scarred me for life. As it was, one of our neighbors whom the locals considered to be a "city farmer" (which meant that he had an additional and much more lucrative job than just bedding cows and tilling fields, though he dabbled in both) offered me a summer job. While he owned some pigs, a horse and two heifers, he was a contractor/carpenter by trade, well known in the area for his efficiency in completing construction contracts on time and doing so with quality workmanship. I will never forget my first day on the job. As we rode together to the construction site, I had high expectations and equally high hopes which included the dream of eventually building my own home with carpeted floors, indoor plumbing, and an attached two stall garage, none of the amenities I was presently experiencing at home. Little did I know before that day was over, not only would I never build my own home, I would grow to fear anything that smacked of a hammer or a nail. Though the exactness of the details are lost in the years, I discovered, even before the first coffee break, that the importance of knowing the difference between a 7-penny nail and one less or more so was a prerequisite for the position, and being unable to immediately make these distinctions set me up to be the lackey of the crew. Insults and humiliations replete with off-colored expletives relentlessly hailed down on me from those who clung to the skeletal rafters and slalomed between studded walls. I certainly did not consider myself a prude; after all, I was a teenager with locker-room experiences, but the fact was, I was surrounded by adults, who I was convinced "should always act like one," so I persevered in prayer for a hasty end to what I knew would be my first and last day on this job, whether I was to be fired at the end of it or just plain quit. Mercifully, the day ended and along with it my dreams of someday being handy with wood.

I admit, my mother ran interference for me, but I did not care. Somehow, she was able to negotiate a new position for me with this less than gentle man that found me cleaning his barns, a job for which, having had a lot of experience, I was better suited. The manure was stacked a good two feet deep and required a boatload of manual exertion, but I was convinced I would rather work where this sort of stuff was underfoot than where it was being hailed down on me from overhead and all sides.

Even though the money was good and our relationship changed somewhat as my employer seemed to grow more respectful of my skills, from day one, I had already begun to formulate a plan to move on whenever the opportunity availed itself. Though unsure how I managed to land a new job, I do remember the day I told my employer that I quit and I soon found myself being subjected to a furious tirade that included guilt-ing me with such statements as how he had done me a favor by keeping me on and this was how I was repaying him. Figuring I deserved some of his animosity, I listened, though not intently. It was only at the point when he began repeating himself that I determined I had respectfully heard enough, and turning, I walked away with him still yelling after me how I would never amount to anything. But it only hurt in retrospect, for at the time I felt a big weight being lifted from my shoulders. As the distance between us grew, so did my sense of independence; I was now my own boss.

My next job required me to pick apples in an orchard belonging to yet another "city farmer," who doubled as a president of a major manufacturing company in Grand Rapids. Like potato bagging, this was piecework, and I soon grew efficient in plucking apples at a rate between $40 to $50 a day if I did not prolong my breaks or noon lunch. Maybe it was because orchards are akin to farm fields that I took to it so well. Fortunately, when the picking season ended and I had proved my worth, I was able to trade my ladders and piecework for an inside job and an hourly rate sorting those same apples for market. I liked my new boss, and perhaps even more so after accidentally pelting him with a rotten apple extracted from one of the many bushels in need of sorting. The proscribed procedure was to place questionable fruit in a discard container which later would be recycled in the orchard, but for some reason, I decided to toss this particular apple out through the open garage door. I did not know it then, but all too quickly I found out that my boss was entering the garage at that exact moment. Peeling the mush from his cheek, he laughingly responded, "If I didn't know any better, I'd say you were aiming for me." Breathing a sigh of relief, I rededicated myself to pleasing him even more. It must have worked, because as soon as all the apples were sorted, I found myself trimming his fruit trees, a job that started in the late fall and continued through the dead of winter, the biggest challenge being the driving snow and the extreme cold. But the pay was worth the inconvenience. And despite being able to only work on my days off from school, I made a pretty hefty wage for a seventeen year old in the early 60's. As the advent of warmer weather coaxed the arrival of a new crop of apple blossoms, and spring gave way to summer and school-less days, he taught me how to trim Christmas trees on yet another of his farms. It, too, was a good paying job, but fraught with challenges which included, but were not limited to, extreme high-noon summer heat, the starling scare of nesting birds frantically trying to escape from the inner branches, blow snakes shading themselves under the tree, coiled up in cobra-like fashion and hissing, and the pine sap that eventually guaranteed sticky hands and fingers which could only be released using gasoline or paint thinner. My continued preference for an artificial Christmas tree was the result of that venture.

At eighteen, college plucked me from the orchard, and to help defray some of its expenses, I was assigned to work in the college's bookstore, stocking and selling collegiate books and apparel, as well as being assigned to its kitchen, where I loaded and unloaded the dining hall dishwashers, all while carrying the maximum load of credit courses. While I did not miss the cold fall and winter weather, I did miss the income to the point where I almost convinced myself that perhaps I should forget about this college stuff and go out and make the "real" money working in the fields. Fortunately, I was somehow made to see long-range that while doing so might yield some immediate cold hard cash, acquiring it in this fashion would be too hard and cold for me over the long haul, so I stayed in college. During the off season, I somehow managed to hook up with a summer painting crew that also paid good money, and it was there that I learned just about all there is to know about painting. Unfortunately, the word got out that I was a painter, and I have been considered one ever since, not always by choice or preference.

Graduating from college with a degree in elementary education, I immediately took a job teaching in a 6th grade classroom numbering twenty-seven not so eager students. Instantly, I knew this was where I needed to be. Five years later, I was offered and became one of my district's youngest elementary school principals at the age of 26. I recall being encouraged by those higher up the administrative ladder to grow a mustache as it "would make you look older." Between going back to school to earn my Master's, Educational Specialist, and PhD degrees, I taught in a summer Head Start program and painted to help feed my family and save in order to send our two children to college. After college expenses and finally with my children on their own, I gave up my supplemental ways and settled in. Retiring without regret after 32 years of loyal tenure to my school district, I decided to shave my mustache, in an attempt to look younger, and now I golf and fish in the heat of summer, sit by the fire in the cold of winter, and continue to hire carpenters to do even the most menial of woodworking tasks.

NINETEEN

Listening

*Honor your father and mother so that you may live long
in the land the Lord your God is giving you.*
                                        -Exodus 20:12 (NIV)

I THINK IT IS VERY difficult, when you are growing up, to imagine your
parents ever having been young once, much less having had dreams for
their future. If the truth be told, most of us probably never even gave it
a thought when we were young. What kid has the time, much less the
interest, to entertain such possibilities? After all, they were parents, and
as far as we knew, they always were. Our proof was that they always
acted like parents, even if we did not always appreciate the realities of
that fact.

But our own aging tends to change how we look at a lot of things,
often making more likely and significant the consideration of alternative
perspectives, especially in light of the fact that now our own children
seem disinterested in our claims of having once been young, or even
human for that matter. It is at such times as these, when my history
seems to be called into question, that I find myself knee deep in reveries
like this one.

Today, I found myself thinking about a time when I was nine or ten. It was one of those occasions I have since come to affectionately call a mile-marker: a time and circumstance that, looking back upon, I realize has made a life molding impression. This was one of those occasions that at first blush would appear to have had all the significance of a small stone being tossed into the vast ocean, only later would I realize that its ripplings still lap on the shores of my present realities. I am never quite sure what triggers such musings, but I am glad for those times when I am able to revisit them. It helps me to better understand and appreciate that my parents were first and foremost people in all their humanness and that it was their humanness that made such a huge contribution to my own.

My dad was born and raised in the house located on the west end of an eighty acre farm that he would eventually buy from my grandpa when "Gramps" discovered that it took much less effort to go fishing than it did to do farming. As I explained earlier, our house was an economically constructed story-and-half, considered by many to not only have been an after-thought once the barn and out buildings were built, but it was rumored to have been actually made from the leftover materials used to construct these more essential buildings. This might have accounted for the fact that the house featured an endless cacophony of creaks and groans definitely amplified during windy and stormy weather.

Dad grew up during the "Golden Age" of baseball, and like most boys who gravitated to the sport in that era, Babe Ruth was his idol. He recalls having imagined himself one day being and playing like The Babe in the big leagues, hitting lots of game-winning homers in the exact direction of his pointings. But his dream was not to be. Born the youngest child and the only boy in a family of all girls, his destiny would be that of manual work on the farm. Despite the fact that there was always more work to do on the farm, there were occasions early on, as a young man, when Dad was able to eke out precious time to play baseball for local teams. He took a great deal of pride in having caught the eye of a major league scout, but Sunday play would be the excuse given to him by his parents as to why he could not pursue a professional career playing the game he loved.

On this farm, featuring clay and fieldstone and supporting not more than a dozen or so milk cows at one time, Mom and Dad eventually married and over time birthed four boys, only three of whom would see more than one year of life. The demands of the land exaggerated by the Great Depression would eventually claim Dad's glove and bat for good. Relegated to the woodshed, they collected dust on a shelf above the pegs where Dad hung his bibbed overalls, which always bore the grime of hard work despite Mom's best efforts to erase it on wash day. Eventually, Dad's baseball uniform, cleaned and neatly pressed, was laid to rest in the bottom of Mom's cedar chest, buried there among the other hopes and dreams she too had put on hold in order to raise us kids.

It was a day and age when feeding three growing boys and making ends meet required both Dad and Mom to pick up odd jobs to supplement their meager farm income, which was measured more by the food it supplied than the money it raised. Whenever and wherever there was work to be done, even though the remuneration might be far from equal to the effort required, Dad stood in line seeking employment at such places as the local feed store and mill, the coal company, neighboring larger farms, as well as the railroad when the railroad ties needed replacing. Mom also worked to supplement the family coffers by selling eggs and performing at wedding receptions in what today would fall into the category of stand-up comedy, something that caused us boys a great deal of angst of our own, especially as we edged into our teenage years.

For the most part, life seemed pretty normal and settled. Everything had a place and purpose on our farm with very few exceptions. The fact that our house by today's standards could be considered egg carton size, there always was room enough for everyone. While my parents claimed the downstairs bedroom, my two brothers and I were relegated to the two upstairs. The fact that my older and younger brothers shared a room while I got the other one to myself, to this day, still provides grist to the milling of their conclusion that Mom loved me best. While I figured that someone who would tape coins to the top of a Christmas gift so as to make sure the value of each gift was the same was incapable of favoring any one of us with a "coat of many colors," I took some pride in the fact that my brothers at least considered the possibility.

Now, I am sure you will agree that every child growing up harbors a secret or two, and one of mine was that on many of those nights when sleep would elude me, I would creep down the hallway stairs to the closed door at its bottom, being careful to avoid certain steps that creaked so as not to be discovered. I would sit there behind the door and listen to my parents talking around the dining room table late into the night. I could not always tell you specifically what they talked about; at the time it was more important that my whereabouts go undetected than it was to glean any news or gossip they might be sharing. However, on one such occasion, it was different. Though it happened so many years ago, I recall it with the clarity of yesterday.

It all began after I had inadvertently stepped on one of those steps I always tried so religiously to avoid. Hearing the step's complaint, Mom called out to me from behind the stairs' door admonishing me to reveal myself. I recall opening the door with a great deal of hesitancy and apprehension and finding myself standing before my parents, feeling that though I might not have infracted any of the Ten Commandments, I had done something much worse: I had betrayed their confidence. Dad was sitting at the dining room table with his hands fully extended in the direction of my mom who was sitting across from him. Next to her on the table were a partially unraveled roll of gauze and a lidless container of *Bag Balm*, something Dad would liberally apply to a cow's udder whenever it showed signs of chaffing or sores. Mom had turned toward me and was asking a question which I assumed dealt with why I was where I was and not where I was supposed to be, and while it was strategic never to ignore her questions, this particular query was falling on deaf ears as I stared at the scene before me. Mom appeared to be salving my dad's hands with the *Bag Balm*. Dad, seeing my puzzled and questioning look, met my gaze with these words, "Do you see these?" he asked, thrusting out his hands toward me as if to be assured that I would actually take a closer look. My first thought was, "What a crazy question!" After all, his hands were right in front of my nose, and besides that, I had seen them many times before. But this time proved to be different. For the first time, I truly looked at my dad's hands. Despite their being open only far enough to make clutching a baseball possible, I could see that each of his fingers was outlined with raw and weeping cracks at their joints, and his palms were checkered and deeply furrowed with rivulets of blood, some fresh and some dried. Mom lovingly took Dad's hands back into her possession and continued the salving as she lectured me on the importance of sleep. Once completed to her satisfaction, she began wrapping Dad's hands in gauze as if preparing him for a sparring match. Finding a lull in Mom's reprimand, Dad then looked at me and in his typical matter-of-fact way of speaking said to me, "If you don't want hands like these, stay in school."

I have always wondered if he blamed his lack of education beyond the sixth grade for the condition of his hands and whether that is why he and Mom were always so insistent that we all graduate from high school and go on to college, "…to make something of ourselves," as he would say, implying that our opportunities would be endless if we stayed in school. And even though I wondered if he had it to do all over if he would have done it differently, I know for sure that he was proud of his farm and never once did I hear him talk about his parents' decision that he not be allowed to pursue baseball as a career. I know this because I asked him years later when he was facing an imminent death sentence, the verdict of an overly aggressive prostrate condition, that would eventually relieve him of his daily routine and free all of us to spend more quality, albeit less quantity, time engrossed in more meaningful conversation.

As Dad's medication continued to mask his pain and drip-by-drip drain him of his life, it also triggered a "death-bed boldness," that ever so slowly but surely unlatched doors seldom entered before and lifted shades on topics that heretofore had never seen the light of day. On one such occasion, I point blank asked him if he ever regretted not following his dream of becoming a major leaguer. From his hospice bed his response was quick and determined, "Not a day!" And then pausing a moment and catching my eye, he leaned forward as if wishing to share a secret. In a softer but equally determined voice, he continued, while feebly tapping the side of his head, "But you know, in my head, I can still play the game." Perhaps his dreams were still his dreams, though time had spent his youth.

While I regret that his role as my dad seemed to cloud my ability to look at him more closely, to see him as a young man with his dreams that he so willingly gave up to ensure the possibility of mine, I am thankful for my smooth hands because I know how they came to be that way.

TWENTY

Graduation

We have no right to ask when sorrow comes, "Why did this happen to me?" unless we ask the same question for every moment of happiness that comes our way.

-Unknown

It was my senior year in high school, and life, both inside and outside its walls, was going reasonably well, despite the fact that graduation day was fast approaching, and with it, I felt a gnawing sense of being swept along in the current of an unchartered future. Fortunately, such moments of question and insecurity would only accompany me when I was alone with my thoughts, so the remedy was to keep busy, which was no problem with final exams, baseball tournaments, and college applications staring me in the face. As a member of the Student Council, I was also responsible for helping plan our high school graduation ceremony which demanded a great deal of my attention as well as an elevated degree of seriousness at a time when senioritis was reaching pandemic proportions.

Determining who would participate in the graduation event and the order in which they would do so was relatively easy since our committee had access to any number of past graduation programs from which to pattern its line-up. What was more difficult was selecting a theme and making sure everything coordinated with it, followed closely by planning for the decorations and their display so that they would add to and not detract from the intent of the event. Having already met with the committee on numerous previous occasions, I felt confident that things were pretty well under control, but not a stranger to worry (a gene I inherited from my mother whose propensity to do so was identified and declared by an inconsiderate pastor to be one of her "gifts of the spirit"), I could not let it go completely. It was against this backdrop that I entered into the last couple weeks of my formal high school schooling.

My final semester's academic schedule was light, for I had already digested and regurgitated some of the more strenuous classes in my sophomore and junior years where I managed to maintain a healthy 3.9 something GPA. It was Friday, and the class was Civics, the study of government as it was meant to be. It was a class taught by a seasoned veteran of both teaching and bachelorhood. He, along with his bachelor brother, who taught math, was an icon in our school as well as the community. What we as students had only sensed then, and since then have come to know, was that their instructional methodologies, though sadly typical of the mode of instruction of the times, were antiquated and ineffective at best—a fact that would be confirmed and reconfirmed by future research. Civics class was all about reading and testing, which meant fill in the blanks with the missing facts, matching words to their definitions, deciding what was true and what was false, and at all cost avoid any discussion involving interpretation or evaluation that might result in unsettling the spiritual mystique and holiness surrounding the birthing and the subsequent utilization of our Founding Documents.

Typically, Friday would be test-day in Civics class, and this particular Friday was no exception, except for the fact that this was an unusually easy quiz, even to the point where we students thought that it might be one of our teacher's stingy attempts at humor. It was composed of such easy questions that it would have had any extra-curricular coach, who had team members teetering on eligibility issues, salivating. It would be predictable that we would take the test, exchange papers, correct and return the papers to their original owner at which time our teacher would call each name in alphabetical order for the recording of the grade. With my surname beginning with a "V," my name was always the last of my seventeen classmates to be called. The silliness of the grades had elicited laughter which gained in momentum as each student preceding me responded with an "A." Getting caught up in judging our teacher's atypical smile to mean that he was in on the game and perhaps wanting to play a role that added to the silliness of it all, when my name was finally called, I responded, "E." The class broke out in laughter because they, as well as my teacher, knew that an "E" and my name were two words never mentioned in the same sentence. When the laughter finally had subsided, the teacher asked me to repeat what I had said as if he truly had not heard or could not believe what he had heard. Having already experienced the reaction I expected from my classmates, in a more matter-of-fact way I replied, "A," to which he nonchalantly responded, "I heard you the first time." The room went deathly silent as everyone caught the unexpected seriousness in his retort. Still thinking it to be all part of the frivolity of the moment, I lingered after class to talk with him, hoping that it was truly all a part of his game, but my heart sank when I followed his finger along my line in his record book, proving to me that he had actually recorded an "E," and I sensed his concrete resolve not to change it. I left the room and tried to settle my stomach which had already begun to let me know that my GPA might be in some sort of trouble. While not a concern for the vast majority of my classmates, it was a concern of mine as a result of having earlier been told by the administration to ready a graduation speech in the event that I would earn the Valedictorian or Salutatorian designation, presently a neck-and-neck race to the finish with a fellow classmate. I admit that I had, at least in my mind, already begun to outline what I would say during my scheduled three to four minute allotment already penciled in the program. While I kept this possibility to myself, hoping to surprise my parents, what I found out later was the administration had also made contact with them on the QT to share this possibility, and because my parents were of the opinion that it was to be a surprise for me, neither of us broached the topic.

Still unsettled upon arriving home later that day, I shared the Civics classroom ordeal with my mom, making sure to paint myself in the best light, and while she was sympathetic, she was also quick to remind me that teachers know best, even suggesting that I must have done something more to cause this sort of a determined response. The next day, I followed up on my parent's recommendation to meet with my teacher once more, to apologize for any wrongdoing on my part, and offer to do some extra credit to atone for my apparent indiscretion, but my apology and inquiry fell on deaf ears. His resolve was now perched on stilts and etched in stone high and lifted up, and it was apparent that no amount of my groveling would elicit a reprieve. There would be no atonement in "Mudville." Still convinced in my deeply held belief that sanity and justice would eventually prevail, especially in a "Civics" class, and that he would change the grade, I somehow found a way to put it out of my mind while busying myself in the activities of a more immediate nature.

Three days prior to graduation, my parents, unbeknown to me, had made an appointment with the teacher, but whatever was discussed at that meeting and a subsequent school board meeting failed to positively impact my final "A-" grade, causing me to fall 1/10th of a point short of earning the recognition of Valedictorian that I worked so hard to obtain. Later, I learned that my parents were told by someone, even if everyone would have agreed to change the grade, it was too late as all the certificates and diplomas had been printed. So as it turned out, while I received a number of awards and recognitions at graduation for participation and accomplishment, the speech I gave that evening was that of the class Salutatorian.

That summer I went off to college to become a teacher myself, having long ago been convinced that in the scheme of things, all this grade point stuff does not really matter and equally convinced that I had taken the higher road. Yet even to this day, when the thought of that undeserved "E" rears its ugly head, I still find myself unable to find a shred of purpose in the lesson he must have felt I needed to learn on that day in "his" class. It seems to me he sacrificed the ideals of civility, fairness, and justice on the altar of principle, and though he died many years ago (found in his shower that had been running for three days) I often wonder if he ever thought about this particular situation again. And if so, I wonder if the passage of time would permit a change of heart. Obviously, I will never know, but what I do know is that many of the things we do in principle are not always right, and then and there, I vowed to myself that as a classroom teacher and later as an administrator, my first and foremost goal would be to do the right thing even if it meant not doing things right. Perhaps this was the lesson I had to learn, though I am still convinced there had be a better way to teach it.

TWENTY-ONE

My Fishing Buddy

Many men go fishing all of their lives without knowing it is not fish they are after.

-Henry David Thoreau

PERHAPS THE FAIRER SEX IS right after all: maybe it *is* a guy thing… but what I know for sure is the way that particular day unfolded could not be blamed on the fact that fishing was so good that our preoccupation with it limited our conversations to something less than typical. It was summer, and this particular Saturday morning it dawned sunny and warm, a lethal combination for any wife with a "honey-do" list and a fisherman for a husband. The truth of the matter is my buddy and I had made arrangements earlier in the week to drown a few worms on this day, so this came as no shock to our wives, and the fact that the weather was so nice was just an added bonus.

He and I had struck up a friendship in high school, and although he was a year ahead of me and much more into understanding the ways of the world, at least according to my mom's estimation, we just seemed to click. While I worked on the farm, he did real work, which I determined to be the case for anyone making real money. Initially, his real work was that of a stock and carry-out boy in the local grocery store. As a junior, he owned a red hot 1966 *Chevy Bel Aire* convertible, the fruit of his labor and living proof of his entrepreneurship. This car not only elevated him to an enviable status with all the guys but also pretty much guaranteed him a weekend date with almost any girl of his choosing. If nothing else, as far as I was concerned, this was living proof of his "coolness." Fortunately, he often asked me to double-date with him, and the four of us would go places in that car I never knew existed. At the sheltered age of sixteen, I had my first taste of "fast food" burgers at *Kum Backs* on 28th Street in Grand Rapids and saw my first movie, *"Girls, Girls, Girls"* starring Elvis Presley, at the Savoy theater. Both of these excursions proved to be pretty big stretches for a kid not yet off the farm. I knew Mom would have been much more concerned about the movie than the burger, and I admit at the time I, too, harbored some fears for my afterlife, should I be taken up while in a theater but not enough to confess and risk losing my chaperoned paradise escapes.

Shortly after my graduation, we both married, taking turns being each other's best man. Beach picnics, holiday celebrations, card-playing nights, birthdays, anniversaries, and fishing continued to keep us together as couples. We all seemed to agree, though we never verbalized it, life was good.

On this particular day as my little Opel, wearing a 12 foot aluminum Star Craft fishing boat on its roof and looking every bit like a child drowning in an oversized baseball cap, narrowed the distance between my friend's home and the remote, uninhabited inland Yankee Springs lake, which was to be our destination, there was not one thing, even in retrospect, that I could point to that would have given me even the slightest inkling as to how this day would end.

Taking the back roads, which always added to our sense of remoteness, was not unusual, especially since I was the guy with the boat. Typically, we would navigate these miles while recapping our most recent histories in bullet-point fashion devoid of commentary. Upon arriving at our destination, we would perform our launching roles with animated efficiency, each man attending to his responsibilities without cues or asides. Given our speed and efficiency at doing so, it must have appeared to on-lookers that we were two guys intent on maximizing our time on the water by minimizing needless maneuvers and chit-chat. With our gear loaded and the electric motor clutching the back of the boat, we would head out, leaving only a silent "v" shaped ripple in our wake as we unzipped the lake's mirror-like surface. Our first stop seldom required a decision as we would usually head to an area that had on recent outings proved to be a hot spot for lunker blue-gill seekers such as ourselves.

Typically, our fishing days would last until the first hint of a yawning sun, and this day proved no exception. It was not unusual that during all this time there would only be brief and intermittent conversations punctuated by long silences, perhaps pregnant with potential topics, but neither of us was willing or felt the need of birthing them. Today, it was a combination of the heat and our taking note of the late afternoon sun settling into clouds, which seemed to promise a pretty good storm was brewing, which finally caused us to consider quitting a bit earlier than normal and heading for home. It seemed a bit odd that my buddy immediately began packing up his gear at my first suggestion. I was sort of surprised because usually such a declaration would result in another half hour or so of angling "for just one more" or "to finish off the worm." Having both determined it to have been a successful day, which not only included a good mess of gills but a rare glimpse of the largest gar pike either of us had ever seen sun bathing in the shallows, we loaded up and headed for his home.

Upon arriving at his home, we took to cleaning our catch on his garage floor. With the exception of an occasional indiscernible grunt or moan, when a fish not yet dead but nearly so would require retrieval because it had managed somehow to navigate off the cleaning paper, or it would show resistance to being scaled or filleted, this task too was one muted by concentration or the lack of anything new of import to add to the remnants of our earlier attempts at dialogue.

Finally finished with our cleaning chores, I headed for home, arriving there in the semi-darkness of nine o'clock. Having tossed my portion of the miniature fillets into our freezer, I then headed for the shower in an attempt to wash away the smell that usually emanates from a fisherman unacquainted with soap for such an extended period of time. It was about ten-thirty before I was finally able to lay my head on the pillow, and it seemed only moments later as I was beginning to drift, this time on the waves of unconsciousness, that the phone rang. Somewhat still floating, I answered it, and the desperation in the voice on the line jerked me back to reality, as if reacting to a bobber having finally slipped below the surface after a long period of inactivity. It was my buddy's wife, apologizing for the tardiness of her call but in the same breath asking me if her husband had said anything to me while fishing. Having mentioned earlier, the length of our conversations while engaged in fishing was typically measured in seconds, and those we did manage to engage ourselves in a bit longer merely involved a new fishing technique or the success or lack thereof of an old one, I sensed that her question was probing something much deeper. What little her husband and I might have shared did not appear to be the stuff or substance of her question. "Not really. Why?" I queried.

"I think he just left me," she cried into the phone. "He did what?" I exclaimed. "He just left me… apparently he had everything packed and ready to go when he came home. I heard you guys cleaning fish, and I heard you leave and the doors in the storage room in the garage open and close a couple of times. He then came into the house, kissed me, put the fish into the freezer and said that he had a few more things to put away. Then I heard his car start up, and he left. I did not think much of it, as you know we're both pretty independent, so I just figured that he was making a run for a late night pizza or something, but he did not come home, and he did not come home. Around ten, I decided to get ready for bed and watch the news, and when I opened the closet door to grab my bathrobe, I saw that all his clothes were gone. I then looked into the chest-of-drawers and the closet in the front hallway, and they were empty too. I think he's leaving me!"

I will admit I am not at my best in situations such as these, and as is typical of me when I do not know the right words to say, I recall brushing it off as nothing to worry about despite a gnawing angst that there might well be something to worry about.

Though I never spoke with his wife again, the story eventually reached me that her fears would become their reality as eventually they divorced though I never knew it for a fact or any of the sketchy details until some twenty-five years later. He and I completely lost contact with each other after that day. At the time, I rationalized that this might well have been his chosen way to avoid an embarrassing discussion of a situation that neither of us would know how to handle. My friend, a stranger! We were just two guys who talked very little, and even when we did, it was never about the really important things in life. It left me to wonder about buddies who do things together but never really share themselves... I assume that it is okay if that is the way it has to be... after all, as I admitted right up front, the ladies might be right. We guys do seem almost genetically spooled to be more comfortable talking about our lures and lines than we are about things in depth, unless, of course, we are talking about the depth of our lures and lines.

LATER YEARS

TWENTY-TWO

Divorce- Readjusting the Sails

A divorce is like an amputation; you survive, but there's less of you.

-Margaret Atwood

THE TWO THINGS MY PARENTS would typically talk about in hushed tones were Catholics and people who divorced. Sensing they did not seem to make much of a distinction between them when it came to how they felt, I resolved early on in my adolescence, never to involve myself in any way with either. But life has a way of turning out the way it turns out, and long ago I came to the realization that life's roads are often filled with unexpected potholes, unplanned barricades, and detours. We cannot say with absolute certainty what we will do or will not do, be, or become, no matter how intentionally we map the routes to our desired destinies. So while I was able to steer my way clear of becoming institutionally associated with those more adept at making the sign of the cross, beading their prayers to the Virgin Mary, and bearing the name Catholic, I was much less adept at avoiding those who make their livelihood dissolving marriages.

As effortlessly as the evening stars melt into the dawning of a new day, dreams run the risk of losing their luster in light of the hustle and humdrum of daily living. Unfortunately, it was on such stars and dreams that I scaffolded my naïve belief there would always be a "happily ever after." But in the light of day, the "I do" unfortunately turned into "I don't any longer," and another sacred resolve fell victim to the fate of so many of life's other resolutions and good intentions. While it is sad that so many of the harshest and most painful lessons have to be learned in the woodsheds of our inattentiveness, I am convinced that holding vigil over a dying relationship is one of the most severe of those lessons.

While it seems there are numerous alternative responses when it comes to navigating oneself around and through such an experience, they seem to trickle down to either rowing like mad or resting on the oars, kicking against the pricks or going with the flow, choosing to live one's life or resigning from it, becoming better or bitter. Choosing the latter of each of these two alternatives, I have discovered, calls forth the least amount of one's effort, but with it, one has the most to lose; while choosing the former of each of these alternatives, one has the most to gain, but doing so requires a guarded determination to keep at bay those uninvited thoughts and memories that stow away only to surface when one is drowning in vulnerability. The admonitions of those who have not sailed on similar seas, though well intentioned, speak little to the process. Few there are who could argue with their logic that "while one can never adjust the wind, the sails are always at one's command." But it seems obvious that this advice might be of more benefit to a sailor than to someone who has already run aground on the rocky reefs of disillusionment and loss. And while there is certainly something to be said about the importance of being the captain of one's own soul, many are those who would trade it all to be the captain of their own mind, which in times like these all too easily bobs along on the whims of surf and tide only to eventually run aground on the rocks of fear and regret.

While such relationships are typically dissolved behind closed doors, it is never really a private matter. Just as the tossing of a tiny pebble into still water disturbs more than just the spot of its entrance into the water, the ripple-effect of divorce is felt to the outermost circumferences of family and mutual friends. The gravity of such decisions as to how to divide the assets and who is entitled to what is overshadowed by those decisions having to do with the sharing of those loved ones held most dear. And while it is one thing to devise a coping strategy, it is quite another thing to carry it out in the face of familiar surroundings and acquaintances.

Admittedly, next to telling our grown children of the divorce proceedings now underway, my parents' reaction was the one I dreaded most, being privy to their historic take on such matters despite their already having been subjected to it on numerous other occasions involving my older brother, other family members, and friends. Having been decidedly dubbed "the favored one" by my siblings, I wondered, too, if my parents would hold me to a higher standard. One can always make new friends, but new parents are not as readily acquired, so to say that I was relieved by their unabashed assurance that I was still loved and accepted, would be but the half of it. So much so that I found myself wondering if I had chosen to convert to Catholicism, would they have been equally accepting. Given the Catholic stance on marriage and divorce, perhaps it would have been to my advantage to have converted, but I am convinced that even under such religious auspices, a commitment of this nature requires the dance of two, and if for too long one has danced alone to music that can no longer be heard by the other, it not only seems logical but practical to leave the floor to those who can still hear the music.

"Time heals," he said as he passed me in the grocery aisle. I considered him not to be more than a situational friend, but I politely thanked him for his sentiment; after all, he, too, had recently experienced divorce. "Keep active, and your heart will eventually follow suit," he continued. For a time, I admit, I shelved his well-intentioned advice and continued waffling between self-pity and hollow self-aggrandizement. But after hearing this sentiment echoed on numerous other occasions,

I eventually dusted it off and put it to the test. Soon, I was discovering untapped resources, and the urge to recapture the wind slowly began to emerge. It took time, but eventually, the sky evidenced some clearing, and here and there a ray of sun broke through, and even though at that time I was far from finding the silver lining, life was beginning to welcome me back to itself.

Perhaps my dad, seasoned enough to remain steady even in the most dire of circumstances, came the closest to articulating the good in the bad, when four years later, after I had found love again and remarried, commented to my mother one night as they prepared for bed, "You know, Mom, the good Lord gave us three sons, and though He must've had His reasons for not giving us any daughters, He sure is seeing to it that we've plenty of daughters-in-law."

Circling in the epicenter of this declaration, I sensed that rather than unraveling my relationship with my parents, the divorce actually seemed to launch a stronger bond between us, reminding me once again that most of our fears are graver than their realities, and that when something happens that was once considered unspeakable, life has a way of finding its voice. The Buddhists have a saying that "You can't step in the same river twice." Though we might wish to ignore or deny it, the truth of this sentiment not only points to the impermanence of life, but also to those situations and circumstances so much a part of it. While what we fear most is evidenced in those things we decry the loudest, if and when our fears become our reality, our very nature, abhorring inertia, tends to find ways to unmoor itself from the rocks and venture back into the streams of life.

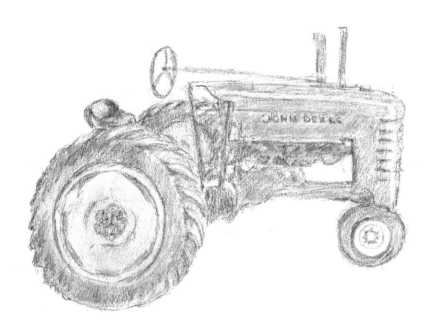

TWENTY-THREE

Dad

It is a wise father who knows his child. But maybe it is a very wise child who takes time to know his father.

-Unknown

To SAY THAT I WAS shocked when a friend approached to tell me he was about to purchase my dad's old tractor would be but the half of it. That '45 *John Deere A*, with its flywheel-start and power take-off option was the very first new tractor that ever set tread on our farm, and it was my dad's pride and joy. As the story was told to me, my parents, believing that you bought nothing unless you could pay cash for it and having considered their finances, decided they could not afford another child and a new tractor in the same year. The fact that I was born in '46 does not even require a minor in elementary math to figure out what took precedence. It was my dad's first off-the-showroom-floor tractor; a year later I became his third hospital-born son. Now, some might take offense knowing that their parents had chosen a tractor ahead of their being born, but I have actually found myself wishing that my parents would have purchased additional farm equipment before deciding to have me. That way I would be an even newer model than I presently am, parenthood planning being what it is....

The reality was proof enough to me that in 1995, contemplating the sale of his pride-and-joy, Dad was losing his battle with cancer. I was convinced that only under such a circumstance would he even consider doing such a thing after all, he chose farming over an opportunity to play professional baseball! I always figured farming was in his blood, and his tractor was the heartbeat that kept that blood flowing. Dad had received his diagnosis in the fall of '94 at the age of seventy-six. Despite having made numerous previous visits to his family doctor complaining about a pain in his lower back, Dad was reassured that his pain was merely the result of spending too much time on an unforgiving tractor seat. However, an interim doctor was quick to recognize Dad's pain as a prostate issue and hurriedly scheduled some tests to be done at the local hospital. The results of these tests confirmed what the interim doctor had suspected, and the prognosis was not good.

Dad was told by those who read his x-rays that he might have waited too long. It was quite obvious that Dad's regular doctor had overlooked the obvious. Always somewhat embarrassed by his lack of a formal education, the fallout from his being needed on his father's farm, Dad typically held anyone with an education in high esteem and well above reproach—although occasionally, he might consider an "educated person" to be lacking in "horse sense." As a result, he refused to blame his regular doctor for the misdiagnosis, convinced that someone with "all that education" would not make a mistake like that; besides, Dad was a firm believer that all things happen for a reason, and as far as he was concerned, his present situation was no exception.

Meanwhile, having sealed the deal with a handshake, my friend confessed to me that he felt the purchase price had been in his favor, citing that because my dad had taken such painstaking care of it, there might not be another tractor in all the land whose condition, given its vintage, would require so little work to get it "pull-ready." My friend's intention was to eventually enter Dad's tractor in tractor pulls, a featured event that to this day often serves as a main attraction offered by many local, state, and county 4-H fairs. I determined that even though it was for different reasons, my friend, like my dad, delighted in this tractor. But even knowing that Dad's tractor would be in good hands, I found was not enough to ward off the deep sadness I felt knowing that those hands would no longer belong to my dad.

A short time later, when the reality of the sale and the reason for it settled over me like the gray skies of a Michigan winter, I asked my friend, when he had completed whatever he had planned to do to the tractor prior to its "pulling" debut, if he would be willing to drive it to my house some evening when my father was there in order to surprise him. The fact that my friend lived less than two miles from my home and seemed willing, almost eager, to do so was a great relief, and while I was not sure how all this would play out, I was quick to devise a game plan.

Because life has a way of filling time with other priorities, the three months it took for the tractor's refurbishing, featuring an overhaul and a new paint job, passed quickly, so when my friend called to tell me he had completed what he intended to do and if I wanted to set a date, he would put it on his calendar, I was pleasantly surprised bordering on ecstatic. I immediately called my parents.

Now Dad was one who never liked talking on the phone. If he happened to be near it when it rang, he would answer it, but immediately, without even determining who was calling or for whom or what the call was intended, he would tell the person on the other end of the line that his wife would be right with them. He would then hold the phone out to my mom, who could be nearby but up to her elbows with baking, washing, or mopping the floors, or she could even be a couple of rooms away; it did not matter. In fact, if Mom happened not to be at home, Dad would not answer the phone at all. Fortunately, Mom answered this time, and I quickly shared my plans, which excited her as well. She added that she was sure it would be good therapy for Dad who, since having relinquished the tractor's title, was experiencing more frequent bouts of sadness teetering precariously along the edges of depression. So we set the date which l was later able to confirm with my friend. All things were now ready.

On the evening we had agreed to spring our little surprise, my parents drove the thirty miles from their home to mine. Like a little kid with a secret, my insides were churning as I chomped-at-the-bit to find someone else to tell. Struggling to rein in my anxiousness, I worked to maintain a nonchalant, business-as-usual exterior, all the while concerned that my dad would once again be able to see right through me. But if he did sense "something was up," he never let on.

Arrangements had been made to have my friend drive the tractor to our house at seven o'clock. While Dad and I made small talk in our living room, I would periodically sneak a look at my watch when his attention was elsewhere, for I wanted so much to be out-of-doors as the surprise approached. As plotted, at precisely ten minutes to seven, I announced to Dad, with an undetected knowing wink in the direction of my mother, that I had a strange plant growing in my front yard and wondered if he would be willing to come outdoors and take a look at it. I knew Dad would not think this request to be anything out of the ordinary. Anyone who knew him knew he had amassed a great deal of practical knowledge over the years regarding plants and animals. As more and more people became privy to his medical condition, they seemed to take every opportunity to give my dad occasion to display the uniqueness of his expertise, perhaps in an effort to bring some distraction into a situation which begged to be talked about, but it was often too difficult to do so.

Wincing and laboring in uninvited pain, Dad agreed to take a look and followed me outdoors, as I tripped along like an excited kid heading to a candy store. Once outside, I pointed out the plant in question. Stroking his chin, something Dad would usually do when scrolling through his memory, or wanting to at least give someone the impression that though it was something very simple, theirs was a reasonable question, Dad slowly bent over to take a closer look.

It was exactly 7:00 p.m. when I first heard the tractor in the distance. The road from my friend's house to mine featured a rather steep incline midway between. As the tractor made its way to the crest of the hill and then began its descent toward us, still well out of sight, I could make out the familiar sound of its motor, unique to *John Deere* tractors of the time, as it registered its complaint against being restrained from the pull of gravity. My father, still bending over the "mystery plant" with his back to the road, peered up at me and without turning, said to me, "If I did not know better, I'd say that's my old tractor."

The fact that Dad's hearing ability was a matter up for debate is what lends some intrigue to this little story. Mom was convinced Dad suffered from "selective listening" and was able to substantiate her claim with what she considered irrefutable evidence. In her defense, often the questions or comments she would direct to Dad across the kitchen table would elicit any number of "What's?" At first, she would patiently repeat herself in a louder and more succinct manner, but later she learned that if she waited long enough without doing so, Dad would eventually respond even though more than a few minutes might elapse. As if needing an Exhibit B, Mom would also relate how a group of her lady friends could be whispering in the kitchen while Dad sat playing cards with their husbands in the dining room, and later, while they were preparing for bed that evening, Dad would question her or comment about something he had heard them talking about earlier in the kitchen. But, be that as it may, in defense of Dad, his most recent hearing test had, in fact, revealed a 50-60% hearing loss in both ears. Hearing aids were advised, but that idea was as revolting to my dad as was my Uncle Mart's toupee. The fact that he could recognize the "putt-putting" of his tractor long before it came into view convinced me that perhaps Mom was right: Dad's hearing was selective.

Like discovering your most hoped for Christmas present under the tree, you can only imagine my dad's surprise and delight at seeing "his" tractor eventually pull into my driveway and roll up next to the house. Idling there, it purred as if in the presence of an old friend. Dad took it all in, his calloused hands caressing the new paint job, his eyes looking longingly up at the seat as if for old-time's sake, wanting, but afraid, to climb into it. We urged him to go ahead as we carefully and painstakingly lifted him up while cameras flashed. Pictures may be worth a thousand words, but I felt that those pictures taken on that day failed to capture the magic of those moments, which for a time stopped and turned back the hands of time.

Cancer claimed my dad a few months later as he lay in his hospice bed at home surrounded by Mom, an assort of available family members and friends, and a handful of photos that bore witness to his legacy. His body, once so strong and seemingly invincible, was now being whisked away by a pair of somber thinly structured men whose hushed countenance seemed to be an attempt to reverence the scene. Watching them roll his body into the hearse, the color of which aptly reflected the bleakness of the moment, I could not help thinking that it all seemed so surreal; it seemed to be no different than if we would have called to have an old piece of furniture picked up for donation to one of those not-for-profit organizations.

Meanwhile, the hospice nurse had begun to methodically take up her textbook task of undressing the room. She carefully removed the sheets and pillow case from the bed and folded them in military-like fashion, while with equal care she removed the items that littered the make-shift night stand, most of which were necessitated by Dad's condition. She paused for a moment as she picked up the last remaining item—the recent picture of my dad sitting on the seat of his old newly refurbished tractor—and she asked me when this picture was taken. I briefly related the story as she continued to look at it intently. After I had concluded my explanation, she turned to me and said, "I can see in your father's eyes that he took a great deal of pride in this tractor." Then, as if in a fluid trance, she carried the photo over to the china cabinet on which perched an old black and white picture of our entire family. Picking it up, she held the black and white next to the more recent photo and then turning to me she continued, "...and I can see that same sparkle in his eyes, here. That sparkle tells me your father loved his life and took a great deal of pride in everyone and everything that was a part of it." Then, as if wanting me to validate her assessment, she handed both pictures to me. Respectfully, I carefully took them from her and looking deeply into them, I realized that for the first time, I was truly seeing my father. In his eyes looking back at me, I saw the pride she had so easily seen as an "outsider," a pride that I have grown more and more convinced over the years only comes from living life close to the land and those you love. Though never sure that her comments were not merely motivated by professional courtesy, I am, nevertheless, so glad she took the time to share her observation. As sad as it may be, sometimes it takes a total stranger to point out something that has always been right before your eyes.

TWENTY-FOUR

Fishing with the Guys

*Nobody can go back and start a new beginning, but
anyone can start today and make a new ending.*
                                      - Maria Robinson

WITH ONE EXCEPTION, ALL FOURTEEN of these guys were total strangers.
Even the one exception I really did not know that well. After all, he
had dropped off my radar screen for over twenty-five years before
showing up again in a blip announcing his thirtieth high school class
reunion. We reconnected then, and if spending time together on a
summer week-long fishing trip in eastern Canada can be considered a
resumption of an acquaintance, I could not in good faith consider him
a total stranger either.

   Despite the two of us having made these annual fishing trips
together for the past fifteen or so years, our conversations still would
seldom dip below the surface. We seem to have this unwritten agreement
to avoid talking about the more serious stuff of life, perhaps as a way
of honoring the eco-therapeutic benefits of fishing. In fact, we say very
little to each other at all. Someone once said that to be able to spend
hours together in silence without feeling awkward is a sign of true

friendship. So perhaps not only were we not strangers, we were friends in the truest sense. Because of our ability and seemingly our desire to maintain this type of relationship, I was always more than curious as to why each year he would almost plead with me to join with him and thirteen of his other buddies on yet another fishing trip. This one was a week-and-a-half long early spring expedition to northern Canada, an annual event for him spanning some twenty-five years. Certainly, fishing with a group this size would challenge what I considered the spiritual-like parameters of our mid-summer escape.

Even though I enjoy my silence and am self-diagnosed as somewhat of a solitary sort as well as a light sleeper, I would promise to give appropriate consideration to his annual invitation. Historically, however, upon weighing my apprehensions, I would eventually determine the cost of accepting it to be too high and politely decline. While I continued to enjoy our annual mid-summer week-long fishing trips, my concerns for this particular outing ran the gamut from living for a time in such close proximity with such a large group of fish mongers to the fear of not being able to excuse myself from being audience to what I anticipated would be the nightly concerts featuring an a cappella choir of heavy breathers and snorers.

My considerations, given his persistent requests, however, finally reached a tipping point. It apparently crept up on me when the allure of fishing and my need for a little additional away time reached critical mass. So it was that after fifteen years of just saying no to seeking the elusive among the possible lurking in the icy May waters of northern Canada, temptation finally slithered into my garden-like life and in a weak moment, I consented.

Contemplating the preparations I would need to make for this outing, my more immediate thought was not to rush to the local *Bass Pro* shop to purchase the vital accessories needed for such an outing—like long underwear, rain gear, the latest in lure technology, and a whole host of other "needed" accessories so different from my summer trip. But foremost in my mind was the realization that a specific day on the calendar that fell among those X-ed out for this outing was in need of my more immediate attention. That particular day marked our wedding anniversary. Feeling a gnawing urge to seek atonement for what would be my absence, I immediately made copious plans for a substitute evening to celebrate the event with my new wife.

I admit that having experienced the demise of an earlier marriage of twenty-five years, my once rock solid cocky confidence had eroded into a less assured shaky uncertainty. Despite my vigilance in making sure that in *this* marriage there are always enough deposits in love's bank account to occasionally make a withdrawal without experiencing an overdraft, whatever confidence I am able to muster on occasions such as these is always tinged with a bit of insecurity. And even though the substitute evening I had planned played out as if it were the real thing, I was not able to fully convince myself that it was a completely successful alternative.

It was not until we were heading due north in my friend's van, piled to the ceiling with gear and food, and lugging behind us a boat equally burdened by supplies, however, that it dawned on me this was really happening. I was not only leaving my new bride for the longest period of separation in our marriage, I was heading into unfamiliar territory with a boatload of apprehension. Even before the lights of our city melded into the darkness of distance, my unsettled stomach reminded me that I would soon be an unseasoned traveler in a foreign land, a prodigal son leaving behind those who loved him to journey into an unknown future.

Upon finally arriving at the fishing camp some fifteen or so hours later, I watched as each of my fellow fishermen quickly and efficiently took up their self-assigned tasks to which they had long ago gravitated. There were cooks, fish-cleaners, sweepers, and fire keepers. While I was impressed by their organization, things all too soon proved the legitimacy of my earlier concerns. While I admit I was somewhat prepared for the binge drinking and the farting and burping contests as well as the near sleepless nights guaranteed by endless card games and the eventual cacophony of human-made nocturnal sounds, I was somewhat taken aback, especially given their advanced ages, by their relentless use of the f-word which punctuated every conversation as if it were a commonly accepted and grammatically correct way to introduce each and every noun, adjective, verb, and adverb. I also did not really anticipate their bawdy references to women and the real or imaged stories of their conquests involving them. And while I found myself fascinated by their war experiences played out in the jungles and villages of Viet Nam, I was saddened by the pain of their remembrances, which they so carefully attempted to clothe in the camouflage of bravado, and the contempt with which they told their stories. I was equally surprised and disheartened by their adolescent-like intolerance and unsubstantiated prejudices as evidenced by their bigoted and racial slurs. I admit I found myself wondering why age and experience had not worn their edges more smoothly.

Typically, I would sit on the fringe of these discussions, being more of an observer than a part of the group. Since I could not identify with their stories, nor find it in my nature to involve myself in their behaviors, I decided my contribution would be that of an attentive presence, neither invasive nor evasive. While it must have been evident to them that I was a non-party to most of their interactions, I had hoped at least to appear non-judgmental. I rationalized that this group was following an unwritten code that would allow things to be said and done in this place that were impermissible elsewhere, and that what was said and done in this place would never be spoken of away from it.

I must admit, however, that while the days marched by in replication around fishing, eating, and sleeping, I also observed some subtle changes. Evidence of civility occasionally interrupted their volleys of vanity and profanity. The relating of their off-color jokes slowed in the wake of jovial banter, and conversations centered on fishing feats and techniques. Energy they once expended degrading those different from themselves evolved into stories of family and community. Even the whimsical torrential down pouring of vulgar expletives slowed to a trickle. And here and there a silence crept in where only words and noise existed before. It seemed like a boil had been lanced, and there was a healing slowly but surely taking place.

As our time together neared its end, things progressively grew more somber. I could not help wondering if this collection of fourteen men, loosely bound together by their love of fishing, was feeling a sense of loss. Perhaps each in his own way was mourning the swift passage of time. Could it be they felt cheated by the reality that their experiences once again had not measured up to their expectations? Could it be that having lost group members over the years, they were wrestling with the haunting realization that there were no promises they would all be together in this place again next year? Perhaps they had only come here to reconnect with a part of themselves, knowing full well they could not stay long. For them this might have been a pilgrimage not unlike those made for more religious reasons. And while somehow such journeys always seem worth the effort, they are not without their price. The reality was, though away from their homes for a time, they all had to go home again.

Maybe that is why final preparations to leave proved to be such a sober and eerie event. On the morning of departure, like muted gnomes lumbering in the mist, they gathered, packed, and loaded their belongings. Observing this scene, I wondered if these men might also be mentally unpacking that part of themselves that needed to stay in this place. Were they shedding the seemingly fictional roles they had assumed in this all too brief time away in order to act more appropriately in those more immediate roles scripted by their individual realities?

As our convoy began its trek southward, and the miles separating us from the fishing camp increased, we began replaying our experiences. It was as if we were afraid that all too soon they would be forgotten or fabricated beyond recognition. Necessity stops found us lingering a bit longer than necessary. It seemed as if we were holding on to this respite for as long as we could, not wanting it to end.

But end it must and finally did. Arriving at our destination in the more familiar confines of our homeland, we bid our farewells. One by one their firm handshakes and friendly eye contact confirmed the sincerity of their invitation for me to join them again, same time next year. I wondered why. I had been "with" them but not a part "of" them, a participant yet not fully so. Perhaps this was true for all of them. Then again, maybe they were just being polite now that their surroundings dictated them to be more so. Oh well... I have not yet decided about next year. Fortunately, it is a little ways away. Unfortunately, there is still the matter of wedding anniversaries.

TWENTY-FIVE

The Plumber

Tragedy plus time equals comedy.

-Carol Burnett

WE HAVE ALL HEARD IT said that it is highly beneficial, both physically as well as emotionally, if, on occasion at least, we can find reason to laugh at ourselves. That being true, I for one should be highly benefited, as fortunately or unfortunately such experiences quite readily reveal themselves to me. The occasion for these experiences are usually birthed in a manger of naiveté by my innocently saying or doing something that in context sounds appropriate enough but later proves to be embarrassingly stupid. This realization, I admit, typically dawns on me too late to conjure up a rational explanation that would allow me, with some semblance of grace, to extract my foot from my mouth. On the contrary, I am usually left trying to justify, to myself at least, that it was a common mistake, one anyone could make. While I admit that initially, out of courtesy, I might laugh along with the crowd as they laugh at me, it usually is not until much later that I am able to laugh at myself. It has also been said that "Blunders + time=humor." Well, in my case, it seems that most of my blunders=humor instantaneously for everyone else, that is, and whoever saw fit to add "time" to this equation certainly has not made my acquaintance.

Here is a prime example of what I mean. This particular day dawned a bit more hectic than most. For a few weeks now there was a steady drip from my kitchen faucet that I fully intended to get around to fixing. Overnight, for some reason the drip had morphed into a bigger problem. It seemed to me that my kitchen faucet might have reached that point in its warranty when it was no longer required to function as a faucet. Unless the handle was situated just so, it would spray water everywhere. I determined the situation was beyond my expertise, and I needed to contact a professional plumber. My tendency is to now leave such things to the experts, having on more than one occasion caused more work for others and more expense for myself than the initial situation actually called for. At least that is what I claim as my rationale for not wanting to wrestle with such problems.

Recognizing the gravity of this present situation, I sensed the need for immediate action. Thumbing through the *Yellow Pages*, I contacted a local plumbing company with a Dutch last name. The dispatcher put me in touch with the person who would be taking my call, and while I had hoped that by explaining my urgency to him it would inspire an equal sense of urgency in him, I was disappointed when he told me. "... though I can't guarantee I'll be able to get back to you today, I'll do my best." Realizing that I was now at the mercy of his calendar and clock, I went about my morning soon lost in other concerns. When he called later to tell me he could still make it but that it would have to be after hours, since his employer frowned on overtime more than he did on moonlighting, I leaped at the opportunity.

He was a friendly sort, and as he went about his task using tools I was pretty sure were not available to the general public, or for that matter had yet to be approved by the various federal agencies, we chatted about his job, my job, his family, my family, his acquaintances and my acquaintances, and even though the concept of Six Degrees of Separation remained intact, I secretly hoped that our familial conversations might result in some sort of a reduction in the bill. Eventually, he finished. Packing up his equipment and brushing his hands together in an effort to rid them of the stubborn sealer and caulk that had grown so attached to them, he extended a hand to me. As I took it, I thanked him, and, as if he needed a reminder, I encouraged him to be sure to send me the bill. He agreed to do so, indicating that his moonlighting was strictly time and material, at which point I found myself wishing I had not been such a conversationalist, especially now that it seemed I might be paying for it.

However, once the faucet was repaired and working like brand new, the heavy cloud of angst that once hovered over my head evaporated, and I felt a sense of pride for having been able to expedite these little inconveniences in such an efficient manner. And three days later, I was even more pleased to receive what I thought was a very fair billing, and as a result of both, I made a mental note to not only call this plumber again should I find myself in a similar situation, but to recommend him to those few friends of mine, who like me, found plumbing a bit beyond their capability or interest. If you have not caught it yet, I was really impressed with this young man.

As it happened, a few weeks later, my wife and I found ourselves at a "victory party" celebrating the successful election of a favored local mayoral candidate. It was a virtual "who's who" of the area, dressed in "Sunday go-to-meeting" best. As formal congratulations gave way to small migrating groups involved in equally small conversations, I scanned the audience, and though he was completely out of uniform, from across the room, I caught a glimpse of my plumber. I recall thinking that such an occasion for him might not be as commonplace as it might be for the majority of the others in the room, and based on my secret resolve to share my admiration and appreciation for how this young man had handled our situation, I decided to make my way toward the small group in which he was presently engaged, intent on publicly thanking him. Moving toward the group, I awaited a break in their conversation and finally sensing one, I nodded to the others while introducing myself where upon I immediately reached out my hand to my new friend and though my comments were "directed" to him, it was also my intention that everyone in his small group audience would hear them as well.

"I just want to tell you again," I began, "how much my wife and I appreciated your quick response to our problem. Like I told you, the steady dripping, which I'd been ignoring for who knows how long, was bad enough, but when that squirting began, I knew that I had a bigger problem. Even though, I could position it to not squirt nearly as badly, I was afraid someone, not knowing the situation, would go to use it and get drenched. When I called, it was so kind of you to be willing to come after hours. The fact that I can now turn things on and off at will, without those annoying drips and squirts, is such a relief. My wife says things are working better now than they ever did." Smiling at the woman whom I assumed to be his wife, I continued with a chuckle, "And you know how that goes, when your wife's happy, everybody's happy."

It was at this point I noticed the others in the group starting to snicker, including the one I figured to be his wife. Searching for a rationale reason why this might be so, I concluded that perhaps knowing this guy as they did, they could not believe that I found him to be so effective and efficient. I even considered that they might be embarrassed by my going on and on about him, and consequently, it was merely nervous titter. So I responded by insisting all the more, "Seriously, I'm not sure where I'd be without this guy. I'd recommend him to anyone." It was at that point the dam burst into an all out uproar. Like human tacos, people in the group folded over in laughter, while the "plumber" explained, "You have me mixed up with my twin brother; he's the plumber in the family" and pointing to those gathered around us now all but rolling on the floor, he continued, "They're laughing like this because I am one of the new urologists at Holland Hospital."

Okay, so my plumber guy did tell me he had a brother; he just failed to tell me he was an identical twin! And is it so unusual to assume plumbers can, and do, dress up to attend galas like these? So much for trying to do a good deed… but in all fairness to them, I admit, I can see from their perspective that this exchange was sort of funny. But then again, I am afraid this little *faux pas* is going to take a little more time, if I am to claim any social and emotional benefit from having experienced it.

TWENTY-SIX

The Unexpected

To expect the unexpected shows a thoroughly modern intellect.

-Oscar Wilde

GETTING FROM HERE TO THERE and back again often proves to be quite easy if properly planned, unless of course you are talking about taking route through the friendly skies. But every once in a while, even flying gets you where you want to go and back again although the route often seems to defy all logic.

I have found that when it comes to things that seemingly defy all logic, some folks are able to explain away the illogical by using such terms as happenstance, fate, coincidence, karma, or predestination. While I marvel at, and in some cases even envy, the ease with which they are able to rationalize such things based on the tenets of their chosen faith, I often find it difficult to go there. Being that as it may, despite all my efforts to live life by placing one foot in front of the other in a sort of matter-of-fact way, I seem to encounter my share of the illogical. Such was the case one winter when, having had enough of Michigan's cold and snow, I decided to fly to a warmer clime.

It all started with a longing to once again hear the crack of a bat as it encountered a baseball hurled by someone standing 60' 6" away from home plate, signaling not only the advent of spring but of a new season of baseball. Deciding to take advantage of an offer from long-time friends to visit them in sunny Arizona, I booked a flight. It was mid-March, a time when even the most dyed-in-the-wool Northerners have had their fill of wind, snow, sleet, icy roads, and frigid temperatures; it was a time when even a one week escape to a warmer climate seemed to be more than an appropriate justification for pricier itineraries. Given the fact that spring training baseball in Arizona was in full swing, it served only to reinforce my resolve to travel there.

Having made the necessary arrangements and booking my departure from Grand Rapids through Chicago's O'Hare airport with my final destination being Phoenix, Arizona, I packed my bags in eager anticipation of weather far different from that which I was presently experiencing. I poured over the spring training schedules with all of the tenacity of a general planning a military strategy. Given my flight plans, I eagerly anticipated arriving in Arizona in time to avail myself of an afternoon game. However, for some reason, I did not purchase a game ticket in advance. How could I have known that this would turn out to be a real money-saving oversight?

The day of departure dawned as the early morning newspaper said it would: "partly cloudy with a slight chance of afternoon snow showers." My wife drove me to the Grand Rapids airport and dropped me and my over-stuffed suitcases at the curb. The frigid morning air shortened our farewell as I hurried inside the terminal to check the flight monitor. Feeling a sense of relief to find that the plane to Chicago was "On Time," I completed the check-in process, and having obtained my gate and seat assignment, I went in search of my morning coffee, anticipating some down time. It was 8:30 a.m., and boarding procedures would not start for an hour. Sitting in the coffee shop, I had positioned myself in such a way that I could watch the flight monitor as well as the activity at my assigned gate. Even though occasional glances at the sky outside the airport window continued to confirm the "partly cloudy" forecast, a growing number of "On Times" recorded on the monitor morphed into "Delays," and as the morphing continued, angst began to outpace my curiosity.

At exactly 9:30 a.m., a voice announced the beginning of my flight's boarding procedures. I breathed a sigh of relief that our plane would soon be taking off as too many of the once "Delayed" flights had now evolved into "Cancellations." Feeling a passing sympathy for those who ascertained their flights to be among those cancelled, I rejoiced that for me, at least, warm weather and baseball appeared to be within my grasp! As announced, everyone was to be boarded by 9:50 a.m. When the doors of our plane finally closed, and while the stewardess mechanically relayed her safety message to an inattentive audience, we taxied to the end of the runway to await an okay for take-off from the tower. Meanwhile, as desperately as I tried to appear preoccupied, the gentleman in the seat next to me seemed intent on becoming my best friend. Despite knowing that we had never met before in this life, he must have had some sense that we had some sort of a connection in a former one as he talked non-stop. His topic was about a new medical procedure that had been developed and was reportedly very successful in bringing relief to patients of back surgery. His job appeared to be that of convincing some of the world's most renowned doctors to give this procedure, with its enormous price tag, a try. I fought the urge to inform him that I was a little known PhD not a world renowned MD and that his sales pitch, though polished and passionate, was being wasted on me. But I decided that in such close proximity it would be impolite for me to inform him that I really was not the least bit interested; so it was that he waxed on.

Glancing at my watch, I had assumed the passage of nearly an eternity and was surprised that a mere fifteen minutes had elapsed since we taxied to our assigned runway. I reasoned this was certainly enough time to have been given an all-clear for take-off. Fortunately, like the best of elevator music, the drone of my seatmate mercifully was beginning to slip into the background. Unfortunately, however, it allowed my mind to contemplate even more my growing concern over what was beginning to look much like a delay.

Intermittently, as the minutes mercilessly ticked away, the captain would announce that we were still awaiting clearance from the tower. Snippets of overheard conversation among my peers reinforced my sense there was something more. The minutes turned ever so painfully into an hour and then an hour and fifteen minutes. My wandering mind was beginning to play tricks on me with such trivial contemplations as to whether my seatmate had taken a single breath since we boarded. Then, just as I was about to completely pull the shade on all mental activities, the voice from the cockpit announced that we would be heading back to the terminal to await word from O'Hare Airport as to when we might be able to land there. Once in the terminal, we were informed that Chicago had been hit with a torrential rainstorm that had flooded the runways, making taking off and landing there unsafe, if not impossible.

Once back in the terminal, I immediately made my way to the airline counter to make arrangements for a later connection out of Chicago since it had become apparent that the original one was in imminent jeopardy given our already delayed start. Instead of my original 1:00 p.m. departure out of O'Hare, I booked the next available flight to Arizona, which proved to be at 4:00 p.m., rationalizing that despite missing an opportunity to catch an afternoon game, I could still be in Phoenix before nightfall. Meanwhile, fortunately, I was able to relieve myself of some physical discomfort as well as rid myself of my overly zealous seatmate. Given the length of our stay on the plane at the end of the runway, I could honestly say the latter provided me the most relief.

Around 3:20 p.m. the flight attendant announced over the intercom that the departure of our flight would be at 4:00 p.m. and that boarding would begin in five minutes. I had already been sitting so long that my back was beginning to chastise me for not having listened more closely to what the sales guy had to say, even though I knew my ears would have none of it. When we finally started to board the plane at 3:35 p.m., I surveyed the line of boarders, hoping against hope that my seatmate might have found an alternate route to his convention. When he did not appear to be among those on my flight, I considered myself fortunate. However, the euphoria brought by that fact was short lived as my new seatmate proved to be equally talkative. In a matter of mere minutes, I was able to ascertain that her concerned passion was not so much for my physical well being as it was for my soul, in many ways an even more delicate operation.

Despite departing on time as announced, I knew my connecting flight to Phoenix would be tight; as it was, we landed in Chicago ten minutes after my rescheduled flight had taken wing to Phoenix without me. Checking at the flight counter, I fortunately was able to book another flight out of O'Hare that would get me into Phoenix at midnight. I took it. Having kept in touch with my Phoenix friends as to my progress as well as the lack thereof, I urged them not to wait up for me. Wanting to avoid taking undo advantage of their already generous offer to bunk in with them for the week, I earlier had made arrangements for a rental car. Finally landing in Phoenix, I traversed the 25 minute drive from the airport to their home and was nestled in their guest room bed before I became aware of taking my first breath.

Despite having missed a "whole day," the rest of the week proved to be every baseball fan's dream. Basking in the sun shining down on well manicured fields, I took in the sights and sounds of the hawkers hawking over-priced refreshments enhanced by the wafting smells of beer, hot dogs, peanuts, popcorn, cotton candy, and pretzels; all of these contributed to the flavor of an "opening day" atmosphere filled with the anticipations of rookie hopefuls and loyal fans.

Unlike airport time, however, vacation time flew, and before I knew it, I found myself having to make departure preparations. While part of me hated to say good bye, the other part of me was eager to get home. The morning of my scheduled departure, I found myself thanking and bidding my friends farewell and heading to the airport in plenty of time to drop off the rental car, secure the appropriate rights-of-passage, and relax with my coveted cup of morning coffee.

Having accomplished everything to this point with ease and with my ticket and information in hand, I found myself sipping my coffee and staring out the window at my plane. Having already arrived, it had relieved itself of its incoming passengers and appeared to be refreshed and patiently waiting to refill itself. Needless to say, I was shocked and more than mildly irritated when a "Delay" was posted for our flight. "What the heck could be the problem now?" I wondered aloud. The plane was right there staring at me! I had checked the weather forecasts, and it appeared that our entire route would be safe from the whims of climatic disruption or related acts of God. Eventually, an inappropriately friendly voice announced that our plane was in need of repairs and added, as if it would compensate for any further inconvenience, that fortunately for us a mechanic was already en route on another flight. Anticipating that my connecting flight out of Chicago to Grand Rapids would be in jeopardy, I found myself joining the appropriate, ever-expanding line of upset passengers bent on rebooking a later departure out of O'Hare.

Moving at a snail's pace, this line of like-minded disgruntled travelers lumbered toward a harried airline spokesperson doing her very best not to look overly concerned or upset with the barbs coming from grumbling passengers. After what seemed like another eternity marked by a mere advance of three or four spaces, a voice interrupted the ever growing cacophony of those expressing their growing stress-filled displeasure to announce that our flight had now officially been cancelled and that we should all attempt to make other arrangements. The line began to move even more molasses-like as the extent of rescheduling arrangements became more complicated. Perhaps fearing the crowd's escalation into an all out mutiny, the voice eventually broke in again. This time, speaking above the din of squabbling passengers, the voice ever so accommodatingly suggested that by going back out of the airport and proceeding directly to the front desk, we might find that rebooking would be handled more quickly and efficiently. Having estimated more than fifty passengers stood between me and an audience with the airline steward, who now seemed to be showing some signs of pressure, combined with my growing angst about a repeat performance of my in-coming experience, I was prompted to quickly grab my luggage and make a beeline for the exit and the front desk.

In O.J.Simpson-like fashion, I made my maneuvers through, out, and back into the airport, arriving at the front check-in desk only to notice that others obviously were faster than I. While the line to which we were being directed was indeed smaller in length compared to that which I had just left, it, too, was growing by the minute. I felt fortunate to be as near to the front of our line as I was but disappointed that someone representing the airline had not yet appeared to process our rebooking. As I watched the steady movement of adjacent lines, I could not help visualizing empty seats quickly being filled and wondering if there would be any left for me. Once again I was stalled, and the level of my impatience seemed to be challenging even the best in me. It was then that something really unusual happened.

As I watched people booking their flights as well as frantically trying to book flights that did not exist, a woman approached me and motioned for me to follow her. Looking back, I was not sure what possessed me to grab my luggage and leave my position in line to follow her. Maybe it was her caring smile. All I know for sure was that I never doubted that I should do her bidding. Walking through the crowded rows a few paces ahead of me, she turned on one occasion to make sure that I was in tow. Her countenance continued to reassure me that things would be okay. Stopping, she motioned me toward an empty counter where a uniformed booking agent seemingly appeared out of nowhere and, slipping behind her computer, politely asked how she could be of help. I hurriedly shared my situation with her while she listened with what appeared to be genuine concern for my plight. I assumed that she had probably heard it all before. Prefacing her efforts by saying that flights to Grand Rapids were pretty much booked, she busied herself clicking the keys of her computer with lightning-like speed and accuracy while assuring me that she would do her best. I took some comfort in her promise, all the while hoping she was not just trying to be professionally correct.

After unsuccessfully checking with three different airlines, she was finally able to locate one seat on a flight that would route me through Dallas with a connecting flight to Grand Rapids. She assured me that I would arrive in Grand Rapids only one hour later than that recorded on my original itinerary, and because everything about her seemed so credible, I believed her. With my rescheduled flight ticket in hand and feeling assured that I now would be able to make my way home at a reasonable time, I allowed myself to feel relief and elation at the same time. So wanting to share this moment with someone, I turned to look for the woman who had ushered me to this agent in order to thank her. But she was nowhere to be found. I then turned to ask the agent who had just helped me if she knew the whereabouts of the woman who had led me to her, but she had left her computer and was making her way through one of the doors behind the counter where she too disappeared as mysteriously as she had appeared.

It was only after I was securely nested in my assigned seat to Dallas and feeling the rush of launch speed that my rationale mind went to work out an explanation of the events of the past hour. Visualizing the woman who had directed my path, I recall that she was dressed all in white and bore no identification indicating what airline she represented or for whom she worked. As mysteriously as this appeared, she disappeared leaving me to wonder how someone dressed so differently from everybody else could so easily melt into this sea of colorful, suntanned humanity, each eagerly traveling to destinations of their own.

TWENTY-SEVEN

On the Edge

Carpe diem! Rejoice while you are alive; enjoy the day; live life to the fullest; make the most of what you have. It is later than you think.

-Horace

ALTHOUGH WE DID NOT GROW UP with a TV in our home, when I had the opportunity to watch it elsewhere, my favorite show was Rod Sterling's *The Twilight Zone*. I loved everything about that show. For some reason, even back then the narrator's opening lines stirred me, and I admit they still do to this day: *"You're traveling through another dimension, a dimension not only of sight and sound but of mind. A journey into a wondrous land whose boundaries are that of imagination; into a land of both shadow and substance, of things and ideas. That's the signpost up ahead - your next stop, the Twilight Zone!"*

Perhaps my affinity with the show comes from my own experiences of living somewhere on the edge of shadow and substance. For example, when I was a small child suffering from one of those bouts with pneumonia that concerned my parents enough to kneel beside me by my bed and earnestly pray along with me the prayer I was taught to recite each night—"Now I lay me down to sleep, I pray the Lord my soul to keep. If I should die before I wake, I pray the Lord my soul to take. Amen."— I had what some would call a high fever experience even though it seemed so real to me at the time. I saw a shadow creeping up the stairs to my bedroom. I remember telling the shadow I did not want to go yet, and as it crept back down the stairs, I knew I would be okay. How does one explain that?

As a high school student, I traveled in a crowd that often did not reflect my upbringing in order to be "cool." Despite the fact that I never drank, using some made-up medical condition as the reason for my not doing so, many of these guys did. Following an event in which drinking was prevalent, I opted not to ride home with the guy who had picked me up, convinced that he should not be driving in the first place. Fortunately, the local police officer thought so too, because after pulling him over and determining his condition and that of most of those in the car, the entire group spent the evening in the local jail. They were released the next morning when their parents came to pick them up. How was it that I avoided embarrassing my family?

Then there was the time in blizzard-like conditions on an extremely icy patch of a four lane highway, when cars began to spin out of control in front of me as if their drivers had all decided to entertain themselves with an arcade game of bumper cars. Despite seeing only the alternating of taillights and headlights, I somehow managed to slip through the pack and continue on unscathed. I read in the newspaper the next day of a fourteen car pileup in that location. How so?

And even more recently, I made a right turn onto a two lane road heading west. Having determined an all-clear from my left, I proceeded to turn, only to find myself staring into the headlights of an on-coming car passing another car heading east. It all happened so fast there was nowhere I could go. The only explanation I have is that the passing car passed through my car. How so?

This is the stuff of *The Twilight Zone.* And yes, I often find myself being drawn into these types of situations. And while I want to answer the "How so?" question, I realize that it lies somewhere out there on the edge of the ethereal. Just the other day, I was again reminded that I have a long way to go in my resolve to accept things for what and as they are. On the occasion of which I speak, I found myself slipping back into the old pattern of seeking explanations for why things happen as they do in order to excavate some deeper meaning from them that would validate such experiences with a sense of value and purpose.

Having read an announcement in the newspaper detailing a lecture to be given by a local college professor entitled, "The Brain and Memory," and because the lecture would be held in a local library and at a time when I had no scheduled obligations either to myself or to others, I decided to attend. In the back of my mind, I typically carry the evaluation of newspaper reading credited to Mark Twain, who said, "If people do not read the newspaper, they are uninformed; if they read a newspaper, they are misinformed." This might explain why most of my newspaper reading these days is limited to skimming the articles for who, what, when, and where and paying little or no heed to why. In fact, it seems as if just yesterday such an announcement would have passed by me unnoticed, but I admit that of late my antenna has been up for such topics. On the scheduled day, as is my custom, I arrived at the lecture site early, a trait I now realize I must have mastered in my childhood to avoid missing out on scheduled events, and particularly meals, for which my tardiness was neither sanctioned nor tolerated.

Arriving at the library, I inquired at the front desk which resulted in my being directed to the basement of the facility where, because all the other rooms were darkened, I was quickly able to locate the meeting area. Three ladies, whom I considered to be of my mother's vintage, all dolled up in what Mom would have called Sunday-go-to-meeting clothes, were busily applying the finishing touches to last minute preparations. One lady was tending to the table located in the back of the room. It was lavishly adorned with a decorative flowery tablecloth and with equally decoratively flowered centerpieces. The table also featured a fine array of goodies surrounded by matching napkins, geometrically aligned silverware, and dainty tea cups whose handles were of the sort men typically find difficult to wrap a finger around. One of the ladies was peering over the counter through the opening into the kitchen, checking to be sure the coffee was brewing while another was methodically placing pamphlets on each chair facing the lectern.

As I entered the room, their fragrances greeted me before they were physically able to do so. Temporarily abandoning their duties, they all rushed to welcome me in a manner that led me to wonder if my presence was anticipated if not expected. Following a brief exchange of names and the typical "Who do you know that I know" attempts at making connections, the overseer of the coffee and the one whose job it was to place the pamphlets scurried back to their tasks, while the lady at the table gestured toward the display before her. She explained in a hushed voice that typically the goodies and coffee were served after the meeting, but with a wink in her eye as if it would be our little secret between us, she encouraged me to make a selection and grab a cup of coffee now, "Because," she whispered, "no one will care, and besides you're still a growing boy." Despite not needing any sustenance, especially of this caloric nature, I looked over the possibilities. I was feeling obligated to make a selection, if not out of courtesy for her having gone out on a limb to infract the typical protocol, then certainly to acknowledge my appreciation for her evaluation of my maturation status, a sentiment often vocalized by my mother and occasionally by others my senior.

While peering at the offerings, I noticed that one of the hostesses had come alongside of me. She began pointing out the attributes of each selection as well as giving me the names of the person who had donated them. The table also bore a delectable contribution from each of these three ladies, so I purposefully declined making a selection until I was shown what each of them added to the table. Eventually not wanting to hurt anyone's feelings, I declined all their offerings using an upcoming doctor's appointment as my excuse. Instead, I opted for a cup of coffee, which sent the coffee lady scurrying off to the kitchen to retrieve a cup. "Cream or sugar?" she called from the serving window in an equally creamy and sugary manner.

Returning, she smiled and handed me a cup of steaming black coffee. It was then that I noted her tremor which probably accounted for the fact the cup was barely half full. Taking it from her, more delicately than she was able to offer it, I located a seat near the back of the hall with the intention of leaving the three ladies to their assigned preparations unfettered by any obligation they might feel to entertain me further. Having returned to their assigned tasks, they still took occasions to remind me periodically, as if they might have forgotten that they had already done so on numerous occasions, how nice it was that I was joining them tonight, leaving me to wonder if they might not be exhibits A, B, and C in this lecture dedicated to memory.

Eventually, others started to show up, and before long two things became very evident to me. First, it seemed that everyone knew everybody else as indicated by the amount of hugging and the number of conversations that seemed to start in the middle; and second, all the new arrivals seemed to have been cloned from the three ladies who originally welcomed me so graciously. As the newcomers eventually made their way to their seats, they had to pass by me, but seemingly they were unable to do so without first extending to me a gracious smile and their hand in greeting, which typically resulted in hand-holding that tended to stretch the socially acceptable time allotment for such an activity. It had already dawned on me earlier that I might be somewhere where my kind, though perhaps welcomed, was typically absent. I was also becoming convinced that my presence might be seen by some of these ladies as an occasion to make up for lost romantic opportunities.

Feigning the need for a refill, I eventually made my way toward the coffee lady, and as she carefully refilled my cup, I mentioned to her that perhaps I might be someplace that I shouldn't be. She assured me that while I was in the minority, I was in the right place for the advertised lecture. Her effort at assurance left me more uncertain, so I pressed a bit further, only to discover that I was in a meeting of the local Women's Literary Club. Sensing my embarrassment, the coffee lady was quick to point out that the guest speaker was himself a male as if such a pronouncement would bring me some relief.

I admit that the lecture was of such interest that I soon forgot I was the only male in the audience and that I sat enshrouded in a bouquet of conflicting fragrances and aromas not to mention a plethora of delectable finger-foods. I recall musing how I felt I was truly living in the moment not needing reasons to seek out hidden values or deeper purposes for why things happen as they do. As the lecture concluded, having earlier mentally planned an escape route, I headed for the nearest exit only to be caught in cross-purposes with those making haste to the coffee and dessert table. Not wanting to be rude, I found myself being swept along by the crowd eager to make their selections from among the quickly depleting supply of the more desired delectables. Eventually seeing some daylight between the exit and my present location in the room, I eased my way out of the line that had yet to take a linear shape, only to catch a glimpse of someone being led by her walker who, having made eye contact with me, was now making a beeline in my direction. Though I did not know her from Eve, and it would be hard put for me to describe her now, she appeared different from the others somehow. Her smile seemed more pensive, making her countenance less inviting, which I assumed meant her greeting would follow suit. As she approached, however, she handed me a crumbled piece of paper on which I could see something had been written, and as she placed it into my hand, she said, "Know this," and then she was gone. Making my way to the exit amid "Thanks for Coming" and "Come again" admonitions, I tucked the note into my pocket, promising myself to read it once I got into fresher air.

Finding myself in the parking lot and in the interior safety of my car, I reached into my pocket to extract the crumbled scrap of paper she had handed me. Unraveling it, I discovered, in a handwritten scrawl, the words, "We ponder God's withholdings or bestowings, and while we pine over what was 'never given' or that which was given and then taken, today slips through our fingers."

Now I ask you, can you see why I might be tempted to slip back into my old pattern of looking for rational or spiritual explanations as to why things happen as they do? What am I to do with this? What would you do with this? Is there a deeper meaning or intention imbedded in this experience, or was it merely a timely coincidence, the aligning of certain planets in the seventh moon? Or should I just accept it for what it is and allow it to remain a mystery? Living on the edge is not that easy!

TWENTY-EIGHT

On the Beach

Nothing is more irretrievably missed than daily opportunities.

- Marie von Ebner Eschenbach

"It's my birthday, today!" she shouted out to me above the dissonant octaves of wind and waves.

Earlier that morning, before breakfast, I had decided to take a long walk along the sandy shores of Hutchinson Island, intent not only to reap whatever benefits I could from the exercise but also to strategically position myself to be among the first to scavenge those jewels raked from the ocean's depths and so generously displayed on its shore by the evening's tide and surf. I had not gone far when I became aware of her presence. Sitting there on a beach chair under an umbrella, positioned about forty yards from shore, back where the grassy edge first made its acquaintance with the beach, she huddled in a blanket. It was as if she fully expected it to compensate for the lack of warmth usually so generously provided by the sun, but as of yet held captive by the early morning clouds and breezes. She wore a baseball cap (featuring the easily discernible and familiar Old English "D") tight and low over her eyes, which allowed her pony tail to hang free along with numerous wisps of hair that had managed to escape confinement. Under normal circumstances, her presence probably would have generated little if any attention, much less a second glance from those who walked the beaches. She would have easily blended in with the myriad of other sun seekers who typically salt and pepper the beaches in south Florida early on any given summer day. But given the bitter coldness that lingered in the morning air and the fact that she was alone on the beach, her singular presence was most obvious.

Starting out, I ambled past her without much more than a friendly acknowledgment of her presence, rationalizing that the distance between us legitimized tending to my own business. Moving on, I occasionally stopped here and there in an effort to more closely observe a shell or portion thereof, and she began to fade from sight as did my thinking about her. More engrossed now in this present moment, I find that the entire scene and her presence in it has been relegated to a place where all my memories seem to go these days, some to be recalled again, in part, a few in total, but many lost forever. Little did I know or even surmise that on my return trek, I would experience something that I knew would always haunt me.

Eventually having reached the outermost limit of my intended stroll and already laden with my selected collections, I began heading back in the direction from which I had come. As I drew closer to my point of origin, I noticed that she still occupied the place where she had staked her early morning claim, and it struck me as even a bit more odd, given the fact the weather had not improved and perhaps had even grown a bit worse, that she had chosen to persist in this solitary way. As I approached, curiosity joined hands with my basic nature that would have considered it unfriendly to pass her again without sharing a word, and so it was that looking in her direction, I waved and hollered a friendly morning greeting as well as a complimentary comment on her optimism. Returning my friendly gesture, she waved and then shouted out, "It's my birthday, today!"

Sensing an invitation to continue our conversation and choosing to do so in a way that did not require our having to raise our voices above the competing elements, I moved toward her. With the gap between us now closing, I extended to her a polite "Congratulations!" and best wishes for a "Happy Birthday." Finding myself in closer proximity, I was able to more fully absorb the details of her space. As it was, the chair in which she sat was situated in the middle of a heart, generously outlined on the sand by look-a-like sea shells. She explained later that these shells were the result of a three-month long collection effort by a soon-to-be groom, who desired to romantically designate the exact spot where he and his bride would be wed; that event, she further related, had occurred just the day before. The thought crossed my mind that perhaps she had chosen this space because it promised a happy karma. I also noted her beach bag leaning against the chair and judged the items partially protruding from it were the sort of paraphernalia appropriate for spending a lengthy time on a beach. However, it was the presence of something else that caught my eye. It appeared to be a small urn delicately constructed and beautifully painted in tiny lady-bug spots of red and black on gray sandstone and topped with a stopper. It seemed out of place—"altar-ed" there, as it was, in front of her chair on a pedestal of moistened sand.

It was only after she lifted her head high enough to peer out from under the visor of her cap and acknowledge my response by offering up an equally friendly "thank you," that I noticed her swollen eyes and the tell-tale tracks of tears outlined by remnants of what I assumed to have been an earlier application of mascara. The lightness of the moment quickly gave way to a somberness that rivaled the cool, sunless sky, moving me to appropriately ask if she was all right. Something must have given her reason to trust me, for a story of sorrow gushed out of her as if it had too long been dammed up and just now had found a crack from which to begin its escape. It was as if we had been old friends newly reconnected, and she sensed a need to bring me up to speed with all the events that had transpired in our absence. She shared how she was a twin and that today would have been an occasion, as it had been for the past forty-five years, when she and her sister would have spent the day together on this beach, celebrating their birthday and enjoying each other's company as well as the beauty of these surroundings. She explained how, though Michiganders by birth and continued choice, her parents had owned a place along this beach for years, anticipating that someday it would become their haven in retirement. In the meantime, it had afforded the family occasional opportunities to escape the icy grip of northern winters, and as it was, planned or otherwise, one of these wintery escapes would always coincide with her and her sister's birthday. But this year, for the first time, everything would be different.

Intermittently, pausing long enough to catch her breath and wipe away the tears that would flow seemingly uninvited and yet so freely, she related the story how two months ago her sister's body had been discovered on the floor in her home. A subsequent autopsy spelled out the eerie details of her sister apparently having fallen and hit her head on the corner of the kitchen counter, which resulted in generous amounts of blood finding their way into portions of her brain where they did not belong.

As she pointed to the urn, she explained that today she was honoring her sister and their birthday by continuing the tradition of spending their special day together. I could sense the mixture of pain and pleasure this afforded her as she alternated between remembrances and laments. On one occasion, as if seeking some solace in a rational explanation for this irrational turn of events, she credited it all to the "will of God," and while I could not go there with her, I soon realized that it was more of a question than a proclamation- a question for which I had no answers beyond the all too easy ones.

The pause that followed her question, though camouflaged by a cough, spoke to me of her mental struggles. "I think my sister sent me a gift today," she declared finally breaking the silence as if still looking for an elusive strand of silver in the lining of this tragedy. "How so?" I asked. Smiling and looking toward the sea as if what she was about to relate could still be evidenced there, she continued, "Well... I am leaving for home tomorrow, and though I have been here for two weeks, today was the first time I not only saw a dolphin, I saw it fully breach!" Then, as if returning to the moment, she asked me, in a way that I felt perhaps my opinion would not matter anyway, "Do you think it's possible this was my sister's way of telling me she was okay and that everything would be all right?" Having recently read something about these creatures, I shared with her that whales and dolphins are widely thought to possess mystical powers and that many people even consider them to have healing abilities capable of easing sadness and depression. This tidbit of information seemed to bring her a measure of comfort, and smiling from what appeared to be a much deeper place, she confessed, "That's something my sister would have wanted me to know."

We both reverenced this moment, allowing it sufficient time to steep into our experience before moving on to more casual conversations that included explanations for the presence of the sea shell shrine, her family's Florida residence, and such. Taking advantage of this lighter exchange, I eventually stole a glance at my watch. Knowing that breakfast would soon be on the agenda, I searched for an appropriate window to bid farewell, and finding it, I sensed a need to make some sort of conclusive and comprehensive parting comment that would provide her with a measure of parting assurance. Thus it was, I waxed eloquently about how "time heals all sorrow" only to realize, as soon as the words tripped over my lips, that the motivation for this hollow proclamation resulted more from my need to relieve some of my own guilt than it was an honest effort to help alleviate some of her distress.

Now feeling an even more intense reason to make my exit, I offered up final and redundant birthday and well wishes and, waving back to her, I walked away. I sensed then already that in those places where my memories go, this one would haunt me for a long time, as even now and from this distance, in my mind she still sits, namelessly alone on a beach chair in south Florida, awaiting a measure of human comfort.

In allowing my wants to overlook a need, I lost a piece of my humanity, and I can only hope that at least I caused no harm, and that by my continuing to softly hold her in my heart, she will, in time, experience a rebirth, a time when she will once again be able to sense the joy of her completeness. Perhaps, it is all a matter of time. It is not all about me, of that I am sure.

TWENTY-NINE

Retirement

There's never enough time to do all the nothing you want.
-Bill Watterson

I PONDERED THE QUESTION THAT stared up at me from the well worn page of an equally well worn book recently lent to me by someone who, given the book's condition, must have also searched diligently for the answer to the question amid its tattered and smudged pages. The question posed was, "How will you know if your mission on earth is finished?"

Having retired after thirty-two years from what I had always figured to be my mission in life, though never completely convinced of that fact, I was not yet fifty-three years old. While I am very aware that "time away" often gives one license to redecorate the past in brighter or darker hues. I had always considered my tenure in school, namely as a teacher and administrator in public education, to be one that "if I had it to do all over, I'd not do anything differently."

But the time came when I felt ready to call it quits. Perhaps it was a fellow administrator who, having retired some years earlier, spurred my thinking with his admonition, "Tis better to retire one year too early, than one minute too late." This resonated with me in light of the all too frequent litigious reports I was reading concerning lawsuits holding school administrators liable for this, that, and most everything. Maybe it was this concern, coupled with new legislation requiring more and more paperwork resulting in less and less contact with the school children and their families that drove me to hang it up "early." Or maybe it was just finally giving up my whimsical wish that I would meet my Maker during a staff or committee meeting, numb to the fact that I had actually transitioned. But then again, maybe these were all just irrational rationalizations to excuse my no longer wanting to run with the fast horses, swim with sharks, or dangle from the end of strings being manipulated by the twin puppeteers of educational and political systems.

And then again, maybe the decision to do so was more like the one I made with regard to finally hanging up my glove, having played competitive fast-pitch softball for over thirty-some years. When asked by one of my then teammates how I came to the decision to finally hang it up, I shared with him how as a younger player I would dare my opponents to hit the ball to me. I was confident that their efforts to reach base would be denied by my stellar fielding and powerful arm. But as the years progressed, the confidence trickled out of me like the steady drip of that faucet in need of repair, and one day I found myself in the outfield with the bases loaded and the game on the line, praying "Dear God, don't let them hit it out here!" I knew I was finished. Even though I would prefer to think that in retirement I would be moving toward rather than away from something, rationalizing that there were an endless number of things I still wanted to do with my life, which made such a decision more understandable, perhaps fear played a bigger role in my decision to do so than I cared to admit even to myself.

Envied by those longing for the freedoms inherent in retirement but who still find themselves unable to make the move and warmly congratulated by those who had already done so, I felt I was being officially welcomed into the secret society of those doing what they wanted when they wanted. However, I also heard their concerns that my dream of such freedom might not match the reality. I did my best to assure them I had things lined up: things that "needed" to be done as well as things I wanted to get done. Golf, fishing, reading, writing, painting, and sorting baseball cards all loomed high on my "bucket list."

I told them I was looking forward to being able to stay up late should something prove interesting enough to do so as well as looking forward to sleeping in should there be no reason for doing otherwise. I vowed to myself to go only to those places that interested me and to shy away from those that did not. Feeling that I had given my profession my all out effort, that I had left it all on the court so to speak, and believing I had given selflessly to the lives of my staff, students, and parents, I now looked forward to being a bit more selfish with my time and talents and a bit more selective with whom I might share them.

I designated September 4, 2000 as the official first day of the rest of my life. And so it was that when the school bell rang that day signaling the beginning of a new school year, I found myself sitting in a local coffee shop chatting with other retired educators who had made this their "first day back to school" ritual many years ago. I thought it ironic that they had exchanged one ritual for another. But truth be known, I also admit to being a creature of habit. For the longest time I continued to eat my meals in haste, proof my emails for spelling and noun-verb agreement, and occasionally glance at my watch to determine where the children might be at that particular time of the school day: Lining up to enter school? Morning recess? Noon lunch? Afternoon recess? Dismissal? And if I am going to come completely clean, I would have to add that even to this day, well over fifteen years later, I still find myself getting up early on wintry days to tune into the radio or TV to see if the weather might have cancelled school and feeling a measure of relief if it had.

It was another well intentioned retiree who suggested that I be sure to say "No" to every request for another job offer or volunteer opportunity for at least the first year "...so that you'll truly know what it means to be retired." Somehow while I was thinking I had said "no," others must have heard it as a "yes," and before I knew it, once again I was knee deep in commitments. However, looking back at it, it was probably a good thing given the fact that within the first couple of months I had sorted all my baseball cards, completed all the fall projects I had planned, and found, when looking outside, that the snow was making fishing and golf moot. Reading, painting, and writing served their purpose, but eventually they dissolved into the caulking used to fill in the cracks around the more demanding distractions.

Unable to draw Social Security until I would reach sixty-two-and-a-half years of age, I feared what then would be a nine year wait. Being somewhat unsure that I would be able to make ends meet despite my financial planner's assurance that I would be okay if I did not plan a major upgrade in my life-style, I eventually decided I probably ought to at least look for part-time work. Sending out feelers, I soon found myself employed by a non-profit organization which saw fit to utilize my curriculum writing expertise in an effort to promote philanthropic instruction among school-aged children. The job also required me to travel in order to conduct in-services for teachers. I found irony in the fact that for years I attended in-services, a lot like the ones I was leading. I confess I would sit in those in-services convinced, if given the chance, I could make them so much less boring. Because I would often find myself in in-services wishing I were someplace else, I tried to keep that in mind when conducting my own.

In this part-time job, I also involved myself in summer institutes and teaching graduate classes at three different universities. All of these turned out, however, to be less fun than I had envisioned them to be, and so it was that after about seven years of professorship I decided I no longer wanted to script my life in these ways. So I pulled the plug again, vowing this time to not only "say no" but mean it! Honestly, that resolve, too, lasted about as long as some Hollywood marriages, and before I knew it, I was once again "recommitted" and wishing I were not.

But one particular commitment I recently took on fits me like a tailored suit. Having always appreciated my educator's role as a counselor of kids and their families, I decided to "hang out a shingle." Like the starfish-tosser of popular lore who tossed back into the sea as many beached starfish as he could of the hundreds of thousands that had marooned themselves along the ocean's shore despite knowing full well that his efforts were futile by comparison with the needs, I decided I would try to help as many people as I could despite the vast number who could benefit. I was amazed how easily this all came about. It dawned on me that life may never be through with me, and perhaps I was just returning the favor by never being through with it.

While I realize that by some measure I might still be considered less than benevolent with my time, what with my fishing and golf, writing and painting, classes and conferences, spectator opportunities and meditation classes, book clubs and coffee kletz routines, etc. etc…, I feel that I am getting better at avoiding the plight of a juggler with one too many objects in the air. Perhaps successful retirement is all about approximation, a balancing act that measures the quality of our lives in terms of depth as well as breath. And so it is that as I seem intent on recycling myself through occasions of over-commitment and under-commitment, I can honestly say my life is actually getting better and better because it is becoming fuller and fuller with meaning and purpose.

So, for me at least, I think the answer to the question, "How will you know if your mission on earth is finished?" is—"If you're alive, it's not," or said another way, "If you've a pulse, you still have a purpose."

THIRTY

Regrets

Every man dies - not every man really lives.
                              -William Ross Wallace

HAVING ASKED MY DAD AS he awaited his cancer to make its final claim if he ever had any regrets, I vowed to myself then and there that I would not wait that long to spend quality time with my mom. It helped that everything was still looking quite kosher on the health front. Having been the one designated with the executive powers and the other responsibilities afforded such an appointment, I often found myself talking with Mom about such matters. While her childlike faith has always modeled the real stuff of life, I would continue to learn as much at her kitchen table over coffee and cookies as I did when, as a child, I would sit on her lap listening to Bible stories and other practical truths intended to address the bumps and bruises of a young boy's life. Mom was always well intentioned and one to have all her ducks in a row, even to the point of having planned the details of her own funeral. Laboriously, she had me pen and re-pen, the entire process to include all the things that had impressed her while attending such occasions in honor of her many deceased friends and relatives. Perhaps, because

Mom was entering her ninth decade, I had begun paying even closer attention to her wishes. And on those occasions when something would strike her as "better," requiring a revision of her previous funeral plans, I was quick to make the changes. It was during one of these revisions that I asked Mom the "regret question."

While Dad sought his response vertically, Mom pursued the horizon as if looking back over the fields of her youth. And then seemingly, as if glimpsing something from afar, she admitted that her only regret was never having received her high school diploma. As a first grader, in the year 1925, she began attending Corinth School, a one room structure featuring no indoor plumbing and housing forty-eight students spread across grades one through eight, which necessitated the one teacher employed to educate as well as manage this entire troupe's many challenges. By her own estimation, Mom was a good student despite recalling the one time she had to stand in the corner for stepping on the teacher's toe and failing to immediately apologize. "I knew better, but it just wouldn't come out," she would sheepishly admit as if it happened only yesterday.

Mom recalls that upon completing the sixth grade with nearly perfect marks, her teacher encouraged her to take the seventh grade exam which Mom passed with a 98%. The ease with which she was able to pass material that she had not yet even been taught prompted her teacher to suggest that there would be no need for Mom to come back to school for the seventh grade.

While such a furlough would have delighted most students, Mom's response was a tsunami of inconsolable tears. Her love of school far and away exceeded that of most kids her age. Having somehow gotten wind of her despair, the sixth grade teacher agreed to take Mom back the following year as teacher's aide in the seventh grade. So while it was one of a non-paying position, Mom, despite only being eleven years old, always considered that job her first "real" job. She would later recall this as being one of the "best times of her life," and in her estimation, one that had moved along far too quickly. By the end of that school year, the gripping fingers of the Depression had tightened their stranglehold on the family's already meager reserves, leaving no money for books or clothes or transportation to and from the high school located some four miles from her home. All of this made continuing her education and her dreams of becoming a teacher melt into the reality of "not enough-ness."

While most kids her age were either in school or working on their family's farm, which undoubtedly foretold their future, Mom was out in the fields picking vegetables and fruit as well as picking up odd jobs where she could in order to lend some financial support to their fatherless family of seven. She recalls that occasionally she was able to save enough money to buy a new dress; one in particular she was convinced eventually caught the eye of the most handsome bachelor in the area. Soon Mom and Dad were facing the world together, and for fifty-six years they worked side-by-side to make life better for us kids. After Dad's passing, Mom grew resolute in her will to survive and manage the farm "like Dad did." In some ways she sensed that his presence was still there, and so it was that she kept the promise she had made to herself to be vigilant in keeping the buildings and grounds looking in tip-top shape. It was not until years later that the reality of Dad's having taken up permanent residence elsewhere finally seeped in, allowing her to loosen her grip on the buildings that seemed to also have grown tired of the pretense and now were finally able to admit, along with Mom, that they, too, missed Dad's loving attention.

Upon hearing Mom's one and only regret and being the "fixer" that I am, I began looking into some possibilities that might address her "regret." Knowing that she would be unable to physically return to school and equally convinced that while a GED would not be beyond her mentally, it, too, would be beyond her ability physically, I made contact with the school district from which she would have received her degree had she been able to continue her education. After inquiring into the possibility that Mom might be granted an honorary high school diploma, the school district's superintendent indicated that while he could not recall another instance where this had ever been done before, he would approach his board of education with the request. Such it was that two days later he called to inform me that he had, in fact, brought up my request at a board meeting, upon which a number of its members in unison queried, "Do you mean Grandma Lois?" He then paused, and then as if building anticipation behind a dam that could no longer hold it back, he blurted out, "Needless to say, it passed unanimously!" He then offered to ceremoniously present the diploma at a special board meeting, at the end of the school year-during the actual graduation ceremony in the spring, or a combination of both. In talking it over with my siblings, we decided that it would be best to have it presented as early as possible given the uncertainty of the future.

So it was that on Monday, January 18, 2010 at 6:30 p.m. in the boardroom of Byron Center Public School located in Byron Center, Michigan, "Grandma Lois," two weeks shy of her 90th birthday, received her high school diploma in a surprise but formally planned and smoothly transacted ceremony. A power-point presentation highlighting her life, an arm full of flowers, a formal presentation, and congratulatory handshakes and hugs were the focus of flashing cameras and video recorders. Twenty-seven family members were in attendance along with over one hundred others who unexpectedly were treated to this magical moment. To say that it was a "cloud nine" experience with all the markings of a *Hallmark* movie would be but the half of it. Something happened in that room that night that goes well beyond doing things right to doing the right things and beyond championing learning to an acknowledgement of wisdom. If there were a dry eye in the house, it would have been hard to determine through all the tears.

Taking leave so as to allow the Byron Center Board of Education to continue its evening's agenda, our family headed to Mom's house for coffee and graduation cake. On our way out of the Board Room, the superintendent pulled me aside. Pointing to the diploma I was able to wrest from my mom's clutch so that she would be better able to maneuver with her walker, he asked me to open it, and after I had done so, he pointed to it and said, "This not only looks like a diploma, it is an actual diploma." Then, tongue-in-cheek, he added perhaps as a way of validating its validity, "So if your mom needs to use it to apply for a job, this is registered and authentic." Chuckling, I responded equally tongue-in-cheek, "I fear more that she'll want to use it to get into college!"

THIRTY-ONE

Changing

All changes, even the most longed for, have their melancholy; for what we leave behind us is a part of ourselves; we must die to one life before we can enter another.

-Anatole France

WHEN I HAPPENED TO MENTION to a friend that I was writing my memoirs, he remarked, "Why? Only old people do that." While I mined for the nugget of what I am certain was an intended, left-handed compliment that sought to overlook my fleeting youth, his remark did prompt me to revisit my original motivation for writing down some of my memories. I wondered if perhaps my desire to share my stories was merely another byproduct of my evolution; after all, I was pretty sure that my initial reason for recording a few of my recollections of days gone by was so there would be something of me left when there was not anything left of me. In that light, perhaps his question as to "why" I felt the need to do this was valid, beyond the compliment that I might be too young yet to involve myself in such an activity. It caused me to consider that maybe I was taking the time to commit some of my experiences to print lest they be forgotten because I am fast becoming one of those "old people."

I admit I continue to give thought to his question and comment, and each time I do, I seem to arrive back at the point of wondering if writing my memoirs might have more to do with mourning the passage of time than merely recording portions of it for posterity.

An elderly acquaintance had the following phrase scripted on the reverse side of his business card: "Growing old isn't for sissies." At the time he showed this to me, I chuckled, but now that I am beginning to live more and more into its reality, I am not finding it nearly as amusing. Though this card did prompt urgency on my part to "get 'er done," it also left me with the realization that my writings would be incomplete without saying something about what it is like, for me anyway, to actually be growing into one of the "old people." While pros and cons can be found in all of life's stages and situations, this journey into becoming one of the "oldsters" is not an easy one for me. That being said, I realize that it is what it is! I have little doubt now that death is coming for me, ready or not. However, what I can say with equal assurance is something accredited to Yogi Berra, "It ain't over 'til it's over."

Having said all this, for me there are numerous reminders that time is fleeting. For example, one of the things I find particularly difficult about growing older is the challenge of learning to use all those new devices invented to make life easier and more efficient. When my grandchildren can, with fearless ease, manipulate the hardwares and softwares of our technologies that merely serve to strike fear in me, I feel antiquated. It is like living in a world, which while it smiles sympathetically, is waving goodbye as it hastens on ahead. Having much earlier made a promise to myself never become a technological dropout like my parents, I am finding myself heading in that direction. In fact, I have even found myself going as far as mouthing my mom's excuse for not keeping up with the times... "I'm too tired, and besides, I'm content." Though I am pretty sure "growing tired" precedes "growing content," which one really comes first probably is of little importance. Given the fact that my peers are at about the same place I am when it comes to technology merely means that not only am I missing out on a lot, so are they. Such misery loves company. It is becoming clearer to me that growing older is about inoculating one's self using a heavy dose of self-talk focused on the fact that "I'm not the only one."

I will admit that looking in a mirror and not recognizing the face that is squinting back at me can also be quite unsettling. To the questions my reflection asks of me, like: "Where did those wrinkles and sags come from?" and "That hair, what there is left of it, when did it lose its suppleness and hue?" I am only able to muster a deep, retiring sigh in response. While I am pretty sure that everyone knows in his or her deepest knower that no one is getting out of this life alive, I still have a hard time convincing myself that I truly will not be an exception to the rule, that is, until my mirror smirks at such thinking. While I was once able to solicit a second glance, the best I can do now is to elicit a passing one. And while I am unsure for whom it is I am taking all these great pains to mask my attempts to hold at bay the inevitable encroachment of father-time, I daily recommit myself to continue the fight with all the vanity I can muster, despite losing ground and growing even more tired as a result. The doors I once held for others are now being held for me. And while I appreciate the "discounts" I am being offered as a senior citizen, it would be nice once in awhile to be carded for proof. As to summer wear, my cut-offs and muscle shirts have long ago been relegated to *Goodwill*, replaced by long legged-jeans and long sleeved shirts. While I once sought out opportunities to show off my physique and strength, I now take added pains to ever so slyly avoid them. My swim suit is now incomplete without a t-shirt, and I have replaced my sandals with orthotics, all for obvious reasons. Winter wear now features layers of sweaters and coats always seemingly insufficient to ward off the cold... and so it is going... youth, oozing out of every pore, never to be retrieved much less revived, leaving me feeling like a helpless bystander.

Like my ninety-two year old mom, who when asked how she is doing would freely confess, "Everything that's working hurts, and everything that doesn't hurt isn't working," I, too, am making an acquaintance with aches and pains. A little grind here and little squeak there remind me that the mobility I once took for granted probably ought not to be taken so casually. Unconsidered and unplanned movements now require more calculation, and when movement does occur, it is looking less like those high-stepping tangos and more like those shuffling waltzes. When it comes to getting up and down, I am finding it easier to get down and stay down. I am beginning to better understand now what my father meant when he said, "In my head, I can still play the game." The mind seems willing, but the flesh grows weaker. I find that sitting on the bench or in the stands cheering on my virtual-self helps my inner-psyche take away the sting of reality, if not the embarrassment, of being unable to perform as I recall once being able to do. In the lyrics of Kenny Rogers "knowing when to hold them and when to fold them" is not my problem: the problem is that "knowing when to walk away and when to run" now leaves me with but one option, and it is not running.

Then there are the issues with seeing and hearing. I am discovering that when it comes to discerning truth, the admonition to "believe half of what you hear and all of what you see" is placed in serious jeopardy as one grows older. Since I am already hearing and seeing about half of what I used to see and hear, it would seem to render the things I have come to believe to be merely quarter-truths at best. Though I have long ago yielded to the use of eye glasses, I fear the use of hearing aids would stand out like one of those electronic billboards in the dark of night, blinking out a public admission to anyone passing by that I really have already become just another one of those "old folks."

Additionally, it seems as if one cannot talk about growing older without talking about memory in the same breath. What about memory? In this arena, by comparison with others, I think I am doing okay, and in many instances, maybe even better than most for my age. By virtue of writing my memoirs, I feel I have attested to the fact that my long term memory is pretty good despite possibly missing a fact here or there. The area where things might get a bit "iffier" deals with my short-term memory. By comparison, it seems that I am better able to remember what happened in years gone by than to recall with any measure of certainty what I did yesterday, and remembering where it is I am supposed to be today is only rivaled by my remembering how best to get there.

It is becoming more the rule than the exception that my memory tends to elude me at the precise moment that it is needed most. Because I am convinced I know the answer to what is being called for, I defend these momentary lapses by confidently confessing that "it will come to me." When and if it finally does, too often it is long after most everyone involved has forgotten why that particular piece of information was called for, much less who had posed the question. And when it comes to faces, which admittedly have always been more readily recognizable than the names associated with them, I am beginning to realize that even the faces are now becoming more and more elusive. Fortunately, I can still bluff my inabilities to recognize both by playing the "we're all looking a bit different and getting a bit older" card.

As I mentioned before, retirement fortunately did not prove to be a difficult move for me. I had always worked to live rather than the other way around. It is not that I did not take my work seriously by always striving to do the best I could while often going well above and beyond expectations; it was just that I had always cultivated many hobbies and interests apart from my daily labors. Though initially, in retirement, I missed being missed and was uncomfortable knowing that the work I once did was being done without me, I realized that I was losing my edge as well as my spirit. Like a seasoned bass in tall grass, I bit on the enticing lure of retirement with its promise of new opportunities without the pressure. Yes, there was angst in leaving what I knew in order to dabble in all sorts of things I did not know as well, but perhaps more than that, it was the growing realization that I was not as concerned with dying nearly as much as thinking that I might not be living that proved to be the tipping point for my final decision. Though I doubt I will ever jump from a plane or go on a big-game safari in Africa, I have purchased paints, a camera, joined various clubs and a meditation group, attend all sorts of sporting events, and off-and-on take classes at the local college and seminary just to mention a few of the things that manage to keep me busy and involved. The fact that I might master any of these activities remains to be seen, though it is far from my desired end. As it is, I am enjoying the camaraderie of fellow seekers, searchers, and oldsters who, by their own admission, are moving along a similar path. Admittedly, though most of what I do now takes place sitting down, I am doing what I can as long as I can to keep my mind from following suit.

In light of all this, and because I am still able to appreciatively live into most of the realities of my life's experiences, I admit being a bit more hesitant about sharing this one last lesson. Perhaps it is not so much a lesson as it is merely a conclusion that I have reached as a result of revisiting many of my experiences and attempting to windrow them into some sort of meaningful whole. My conclusion is that such gleanings have led to a "change" in my thinking.

While some may claim that this change could just as easily be attributed to the fact that I am growing older, I cannot really be sure if it is a byproduct of natural evolution or if, over the years, I have just grown more convinced that life is teaching me to be less certain about certain things.

I admit that the reason for my hesitancy in sharing this "change" is my fear of being judged without being able to further explain or defend myself. But growing more and more convinced that my memoirs would be incomplete without its inclusion, I have decided to go ahead and share this last life "changing" lesson.

As with my lament concerning the passage of time and ultimately my own passage, this particular sharing is deeply personal. While I will never claim that this is just how things are in the "natural" scheme of things, it is just how things have been in the scheme of things for me. I am convinced that ultimately everyone will travel his or her own singular path to extinction.

Having qualified all this, it is now time to talk about the elephant in the room. There is little doubt in my mind that the most influential building blocks of my life have been and in many ways continue to be scaffolded on "Belief." More specifically, that is "Belief" in the Christian sense of The Word.

The stories I heard from the Bible while sitting on my mom's lap and at the feet of my Sunday school teachers not only provided me with childhood entertainment but also with a sense of wonderment and awe that would rival any Hollywood trilogy. Never for a moment did I consider that the waters may not have parted without the use of a light-saber, that the whale had not actually downed a McJonah, or that a star actually hung over a stable where a newborn baby lay in a feeding trough while angels fluttered above flocks of skittish sheep on nearby hillsides, and yet a part of me always wondered how could all of this be possible, and why was it something that only happened long ago? Perhaps it is just another downside to aging, but while these stories still provide me with the standards by which I tend to measure my behaviors, I am giving myself permission to entertain the thought that perhaps these stories are more fiction than fact, more allegorical than actual. Said another way, I readily admit I entertain doubts concerning the jot-and-tittle of these Biblically recorded stories. Such uncertainty, I will admit, causes me to lament the loss of childhood innocence with its undeniable certainty. On the other hand, an upside might be that though I continue to judge some of my behaviors to be "good" while fearing others might be in need of redemption, if not a full measure of mercy tamped down and overflowing, I still find myself salting and peppering my conversations with the axioms and adages derived from many of those same Biblical stories, albeit I now use them more liberally to drive home a point in support of a particular position or argument. So what am I trying to say here? I guess if the entire onion is to be peeled, I weep over my loss of child-like faith having now come to the point of no longer being able to believe in the God of my childhood.

Viewed from where I sit today, I realize that while I was growing up, mine was a "Santa Claus"-God. If I needed or just wanted something, all I had to do was make my request, preferably on bended knee with eyes closed and head titled slightly upward. If I was confessing something for which I was seeking forgiveness, it too required a bended knee and closed eyes, but for this prayer, it seemed more reverent to bow my head. I was convinced that whether or not any of my requests were honored depended on how earnest and sincere I was in asking. It also was dependent on God's checking His list to see if I had been naughty or nice. It led me to conclude that He was always looking over my shoulder with a clipboard in hand, recording my every performance, which would eventually be used to determine whether or not I would make the traveling squad. Fear and guilt combined to "keep me in line" or at least out of the sort of serious trouble that would embarrass my parents. While passing up many an opportunity to "sin," my motivation for doing so was to obtain the short-term reward of staying out of jail and the long-term reward of staying out of hell. Interestingly, though, despite toeing the line, I was taught that I should never assume that even my very best efforts would be enough to guarantee me a place in heaven. Consequently, I was always looking for ways to be better and feeling guilty when I would judge myself falling short. Pulpit-ed preachers, high and lifted up, with their pounding fists and angry voices hawking my need for repentance merely perpetuated this child-like angst. And though I did not realize it at the time, their convictions, anchored in undeniable certainty, would become the very thing that would begin the process of unmooring and eroding the footings of mine. After all, can we know anything about God unless we know that we cannot truly know Him?

While my college experience opened more than a few doors for me, hinting at other ways of look at things, responsibilities took center stage, and such deeper thinking and questioning were often relegated to the category of passing thoughts. Marriage and children seemed to beg for something solid and dependable, and so almost effortlessly, things continued as they had always been, passed down from previous generations; after all, it was just how things were done and "not ours to question why." My children were raised, as was I, under the watchful eye of a "judgmental God." While this apparently proved successful, as my children toed the line and brought only respect and pride to our family, I now have this gnawing sense that I might have short-changed them in order to assuage my own need for security and certainty. The sense of pride I once felt for a job well done has turned to a kind of sadness I cannot explain. My personal journey has brought many "changes" in my thinking, leaving me to lament my inability to "believe" or at least to do so in the same way I once did.

Though many there are who are convinced, beyond their need for faith, that they are counted among the "ins" and will merit the heaven in the sky because they have not only confessed and "repented," but now live a certain way here on earth as dictated by their chosen or inherited religion, I find myself less sure, though I try not to wear my doubt as a badge of courage. I am hoping the beatitude in this regard is very intentional in its blessing of those who "seek" rather than those who are convinced there is no need to do so; the blessing of those who "hunger and thirst" rather than those who consider themselves fully sated. Granted, it is far more difficult to live in the questions than the answers; it is more difficult to live in mystery than to live in certainty, especially when it comes to such things as heaven and hell. When questioned what I believe about such ethereal states, I tend to hold hands with the awe-ist in that while I care deeply, I just do not know; I can only stand in awe of the unknown. Like Martin Luther's take on the matter of whether there exists a heaven and a hell, he said, "I feel that it is a God-thing." I cannot do away with my uncertainty by merely choosing to be certain. Has believing ever made anything so? If that were the case, would not the Chicago Cubs have won a World Series long ago based solely on the optimistic, finger-crossing, unwaveringly tenacious faith of their "Opening Day" fans?

There is a part of me that would like to believe I am not alone in my thinking though I wonder if there is much "safety in numbers" in matters such as this. Another part of me would like to believe that what I am going through is just a natural process, for as it says in 1 Corinthians 13:11 (NIV) *"When I was a child, I talked like a child, I thought like a child, I reasoned like a child. When I became a man, I put the ways of childhood behind me."* While I cannot be sure of what I have gained by evolving in this manner, I do admit lamenting what I might have lost. Unlike so many others, more and more I find myself unable to provide quick and easy answers to life's questions. I find myself much less able to relegate such things as devastating earthquakes, tornadoes, and tsunamis to the "will of God." Ironically, the cords of such certainty about God's interventions and intentions that I once held so innocently and yet so firmly in my grasp are now unraveling and slipping through my fingers just at the point when my life is ebbing and when having something to hold onto could provide me with a measure of comfort. I did not choose to loosen my grasp; the rope just went limp, and along with it, my confidence in the literalism and inerrancy of Scripture which is for me now morphing into less stringent protocol. I have grown weary and wary of those who use their "God-given call" to demystify the mystery based on their interpretations and predicated on their creeds and calendars. There seems to be something egotistical about reducing God to something or someone who can be observed and completely understood. No, I am now finding that if I am ever to be okay with all this stuff again, I will need to find a way to live in the awe-filled mystery of not knowing anything for sure.

I suppose, if it were important that I be placed into some sort of ideological box, I would say that I now fall in with those more "spiritual" than "religious" though I cannot be sure that my being more "spiritual" now did not have a lot to do with my having been brought up more "religious" then. All I know for sure is that I can no longer depend solely on doctrine or dogma or passionate mentors to direct my path. Mine has become a personal pursuit of truth, an "inside" communion with a God who historically I had relegated to the "outside." Admittedly, I am not sure I would recognize truth even if I encountered it. Perhaps that is why I have decided to look for my peace and contentment by living in and into the mystery. Besides, I am pretty sure that truth is probably bigger than I or anyone else could possibly ever imagine anyway.

Well, there it is; the underbelly of who I was and who I have become. Who or what I will be tomorrow is all part of the mystery. All I know for sure is that as I am moving into the later stages of my life, I am becoming more content with not having to know. Living in the moment—not needing to fully understand what my past might have taught me or needing to fret over what my unknowable future might still teach me—brings me a "peace that passes all understanding." The peace that comes from realizing some things might not ever be fully comprehended nor do they need to be.

In conclusion, while it has been my hope all along that by sharing some of my life stories with you, you might get to know me better, I also hope that by doing so, you might be inspired to take a brief look back at your own life stories. Perhaps they hold lessons for you as well. Be open to them and willing to assume the responsibility for changes in your own thinking. And through it all, know that you are not alone. In fact, none of us have ever been alone. We are all children of the mystery. We are all children of God.

Namaste,
Denn